50

CW01659006

The 500 Hidden Secrets of

PRAGUE

INTRODUCTION

This guide book invites you to leave the beaten track behind and explore unknown, surprising places in Prague. It aims to supplement the information that is typically found in guidebooks and show readers another dimension of the city. From the best places to enjoy a tasty breakfast or brunch, to relaxing walks and unexpected shortcuts, sweet guilty pleasures, great coffee bars and places to have food for (cultural) thought. Explore hidden corners in the city centre where you can witness the city's glorious past, and beyond – where today's inhabitants live, work and play.

The 500 Hidden Secrets of Prague has all the ingredients for an intimate rendezvous with the city, appealing to all kinds of travellers and city dwellers. It makes for an interesting read whether you are looking to enhance your weekend city trip or your year-round expat life. Find tips on how to get the most out of your stay if you are on a tight budget, but also on how to indulge yourself if you believe the sky is the limit.

Finally, this guide does not provide an exhaustive list of everything there is to see and do in this vibrant city as that would be simply impossible. Think of it instead as a set of personal recommendations that are based on experience and which will hopefully please and surprise you. The author shares her favourite spots with readers, much as she would do with a friend who is interested in visiting Prague.

HOW TO USE THIS BOOK?

This guide lists 500 things you need to know about Prague in 100 different categories. Most of these are places to visit, with practical information to help you find your way. Others are bits of information that help you get to know the city and its habitants. The aim of this guide is to inspire, not to cover the city from A to Z.

The places listed in the guide are given an address, including the neighbourhood (for example Vinohrady or Lesser Town), and a number. The neighbourhood and number allow you to find the locations on the maps at the beginning of the book: first look for the map of the corresponding neighbourhood, then look for the right number. A word of caution however: these maps are not detailed enough to allow you to find specific locations in the city. You can obtain an excellent map from any tourist office or in most hotels. Or the addresses can be located on a smartphone.

Please also bear in mind that cities change all the time. The chef who hits a high note one day may be uninspiring on the day you happen to visit. The hotel ecstatically reviewed in this book might suddenly go downhill under a new manager. The bar considered one of the 5 great places for jazz and blues might be empty on the night you visit. This is obviously a highly personal selection. You might not always agree with it. If you want to leave a comment, recommend a bar or reveal your favourite secret place, please visit the website *www.the500hiddensecrets.com* – you'll also find free tips and the latest news about the series there – or follow *@500hiddensecrets* on Instagram or Facebook and leave a comment.

THE AUTHOR

Vendula Havlikova spent the most interesting years of her young life in Prague studying to get her journalism degree. On the weekends, she explored the city, camera in hand, from top to bottom, discovering everything it had to offer. Not taking the city for granted and maintaining some distance allowed her to keep an open mind as she roamed around. That is how Prague became like a second home to her, and she still likes to visit it frequently on what she calls one of her 'homecations', that are dedicated to (re)discovering Prague. Besides her full-time job at the European Parliament, Vendula is also an aspiring writer and a freelance journalist, contributing to various online lifestyle, travel and political magazines.

The author is convinced this city has very desirable qualities, both for a short visit as well as for a lifetime and hopes travellers and new arrivals make the best out of their urban experience. She hopes they will throw away their selfie sticks and come round to the principles of slow travel, learning that mental pictures and sentient moments make memories more durable.

Vendula would like to thank Tomas Wehle, Filip Havlik and Jiri Ryba for their enthusiastic contributions to the project, as well as all her other friends who were willing to share their secret tips. And, last but not least, her beloved husband Sander Couvreur for all his patience.

PRAGUE

overview

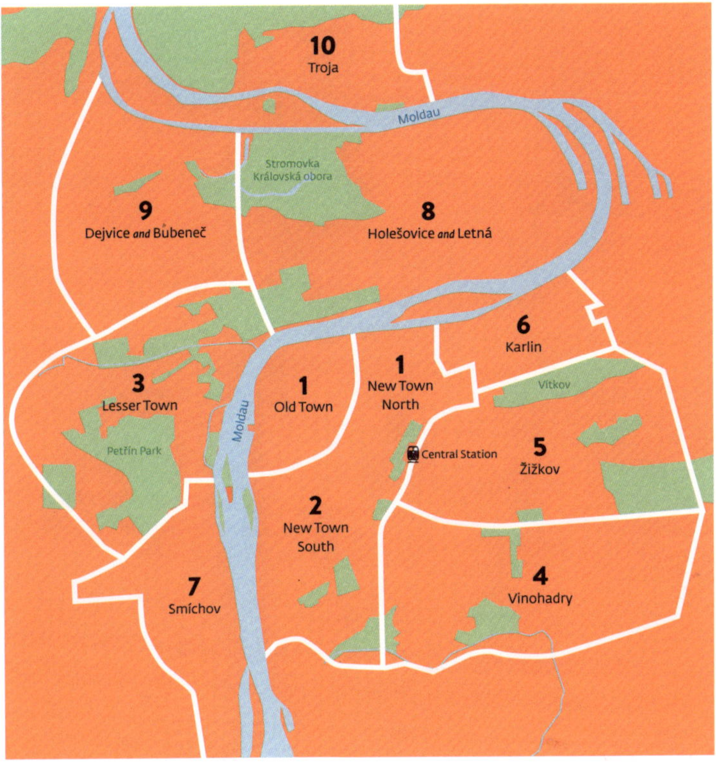

Map 1

OLD TOWN *and* NEW TOWN NORTH

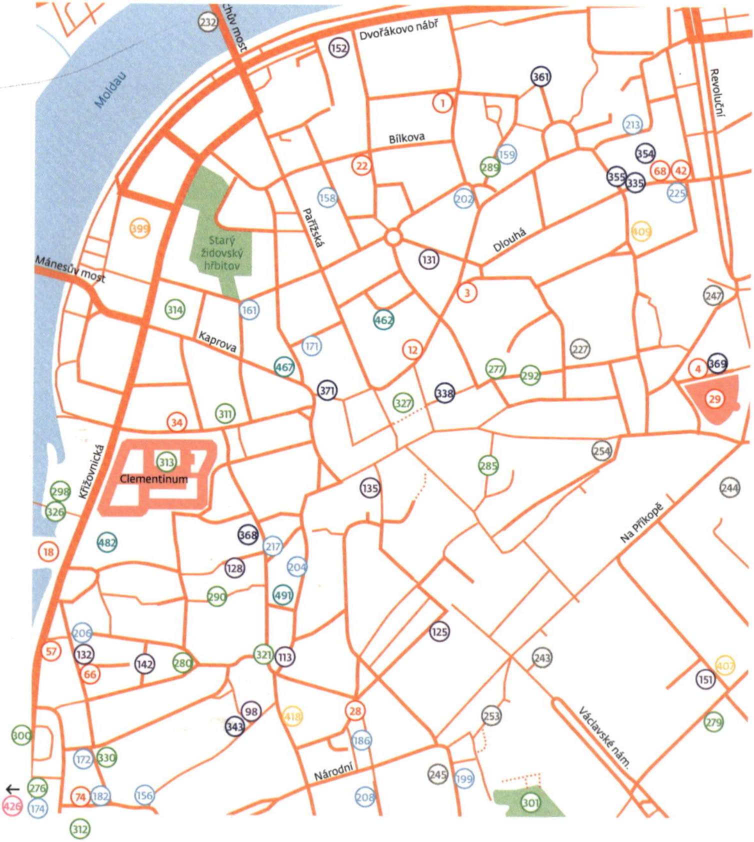

EAT – DRINK – SHOP – BUILDINGS – DISCOVER – CULTURE – CHILDREN – SLEEP – WEEKEND ACTIVITIES – RANDOM

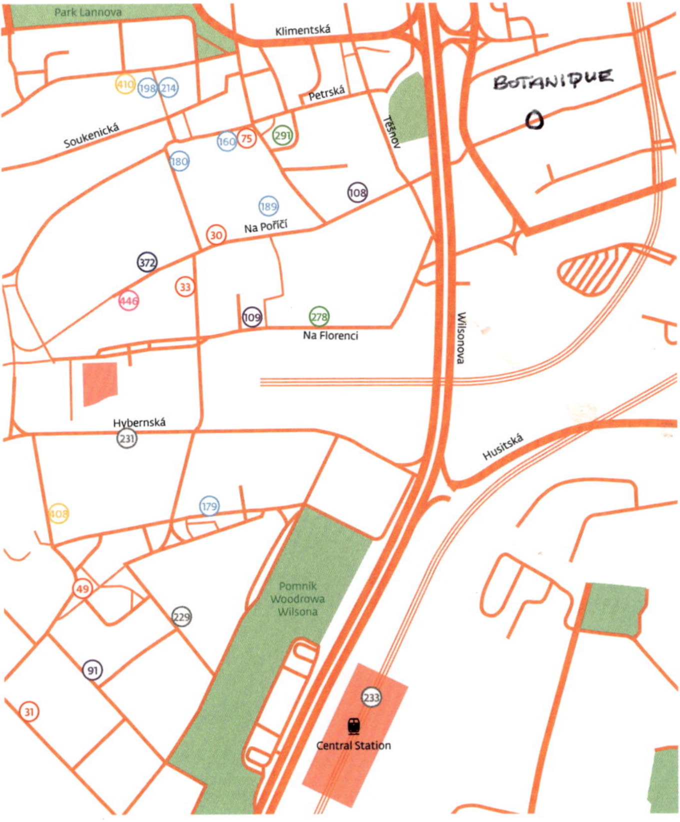

EAT – DRINK – SHOP – BUILDINGS – DISCOVER – CULTURE – CHILDREN – SLEEP – WEEKEND ACTIVITIES – RANDOM

Map 2

NEW TOWN SOUTH

EAT – DRINK – SHOP – BUILDINGS – DISCOVER – CULTURE – CHILDREN – SLEEP – WEEKEND ACTIVITIES – RANDOM

Map 3
LESSER TOWN

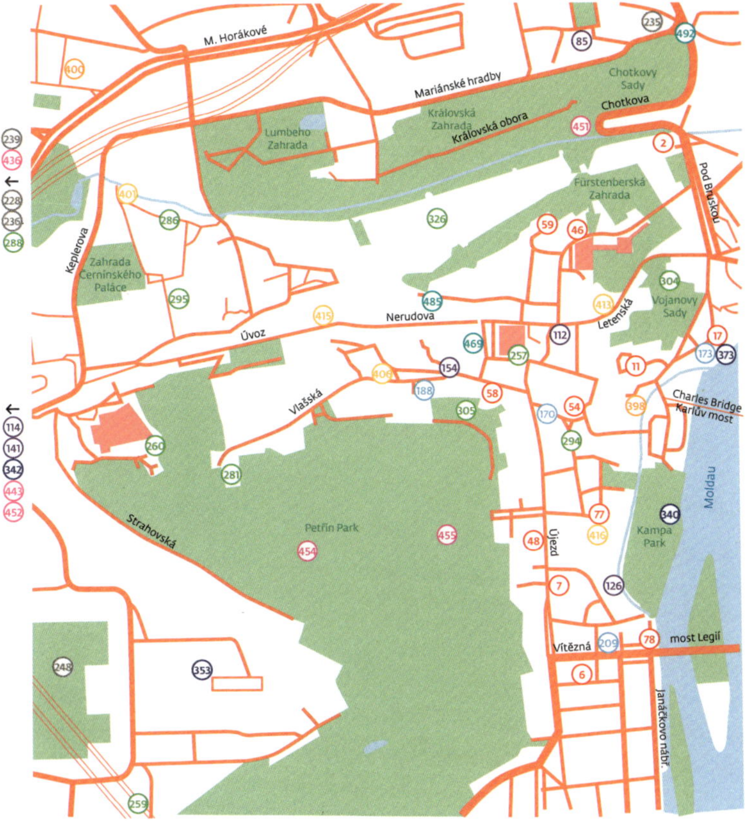

EAT – DRINK – SHOP – BUILDINGS – DISCOVER – CULTURE – CHILDREN – SLEEP – WEEKEND ACTIVITIES – RANDOM

Map 4
VINOHRADY

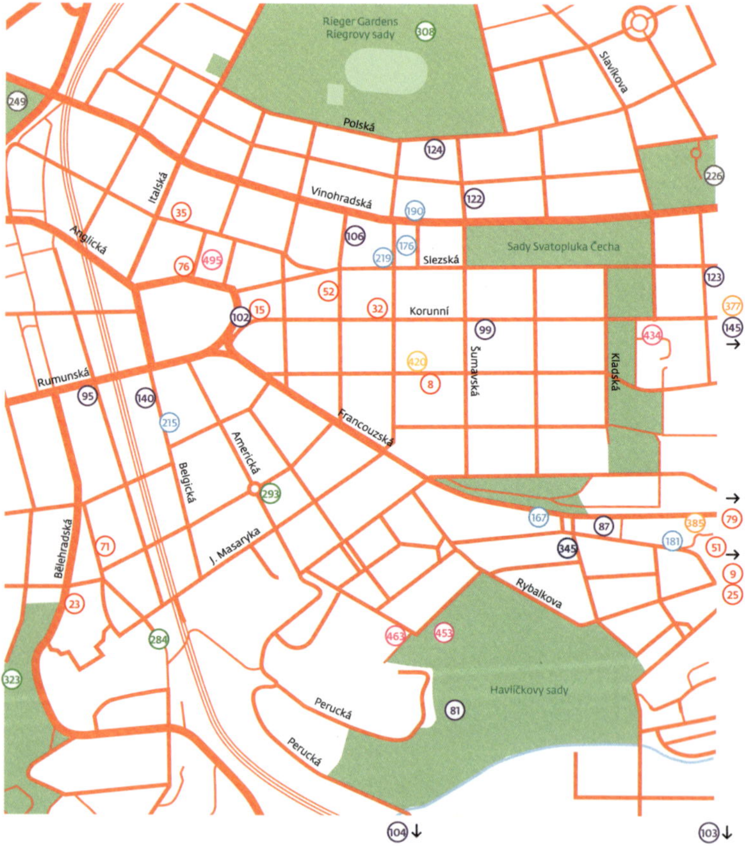

EAT – DRINK – SHOP – BUILDINGS – DISCOVER – CULTURE – CHILDREN – SLEEP – WEEKEND ACTIVITIES – RANDOM

Map 5
ŽIŽKOV

EAT – DRINK – SHOP – BUILDINGS – DISCOVER – CULTURE – CHILDREN – SLEEP – WEEKEND ACTIVITIES – RANDOM

Map 6

KARLÍN

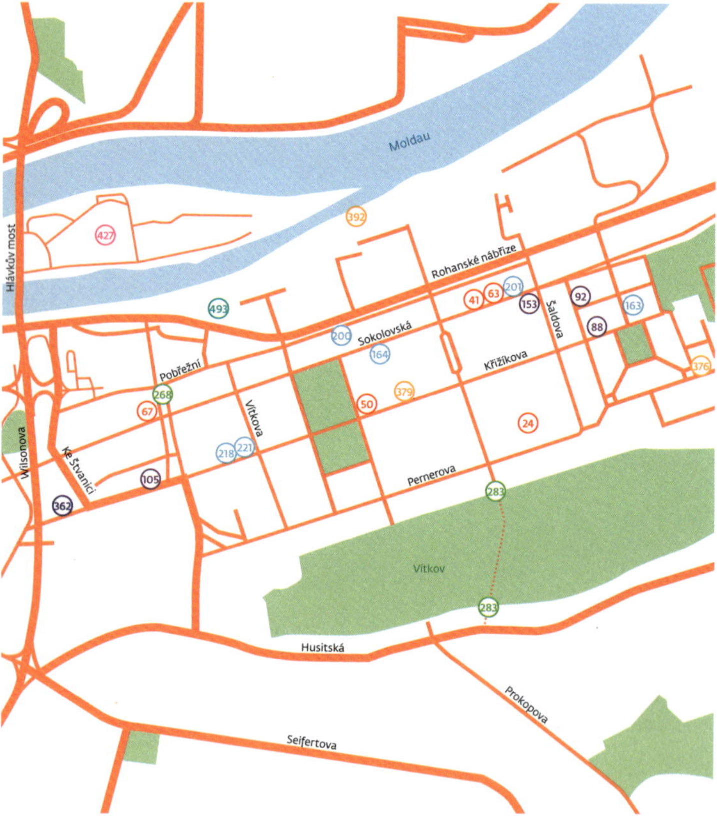

EAT – DRINK – SHOP – BUILDINGS – DISCOVER – CULTURE – CHILDREN – SLEEP – WEEKEND ACTIVITIES – RANDOM

Map 7
SMÍCHOV

EAT – DRINK – SHOP – BUILDINGS – DISCOVER – CULTURE – CHILDREN – SLEEP – WEEKEND ACTIVITIES – RANDOM

Map 8
HOLEŠOVICE
and LETNÁ

EAT – DRINK – SHOP – BUILDINGS – DISCOVER – CULTURE – CHILDREN – SLEEP – WEEKEND ACTIVITIES – RANDOM

EAT – DRINK – SHOP – BUILDINGS – DISCOVER – CULTURE – CHILDREN – SLEEP – WEEKEND ACTIVITIES – RANDOM

Map 9

DEJVICE and BUBENEČ

EAT – DRINK – SHOP – BUILDINGS – DISCOVER – CULTURE – CHILDREN – SLEEP – WEEKEND ACTIVITIES – RANDOM

Map 10

TROJA

EAT – DRINK – SHOP – BUILDINGS – DISCOVER – CULTURE – CHILDREN – SLEEP – WEEKEND ACTIVITIES – RANDOM

BISTRO 8

80 PLACES TO EAT OR BUY GOOD FOOD

5 of the CLASSIEST RESTAURANTS

1 **FIELD**
U Milosrdných 12
Old Town ①
+420 222 316 999
fieldrestaurant.cz

Michelin-starred chef Radek Kašpárek's team often ventures out into the forest where they gather plants and herbs to create mind-blowing, intricate dishes. Book a table to experience dishes presented on moss and potions with cold pine cone smoke. In between courses try to spot the field animals on the spectacular ceiling.

2 **VILLA RICHTER**
Staré zámecké schody 6
Lesser Town ③
+420 702 205 108
villarichter.cz

Located at the foot of Castle Hill, Piano Nobile in Villa Richter is the perfect place for a special occasion. Book a table in the winter garden (a breezy terrace in the summer), which overlooks Prague's rooftops and Saint Wenceslas's vineyard. Here Bohemia's patron saint is said to have sown the seeds for his own wine, laying the foundation of Czech winemaking.

3 **KALINA**

Dlouhá 12
Old Town ①
+420 222 317 715
kalinarestaurant.cz

The menu of this elegant restaurant under Baroque vaulted ceilings can include anything from snails to grilled veal sweetbreads. But regardless of what you are served, you will be blown away by the quality of this passionate chef's cooking and of the sommelier's wine-pairing recommendations. The lunch menu changes daily. In the evening, you can only order the tasting menu.

4 **SARAH BERNHARDT RESTAURANT**

U Obecního domu 1
Old Town ①
+420 222 195 900
hotel-paris.cz

The exquisite Art Nouveau interior – blue split glass mosaics, original lighting fixtures, inlaid panelling and gilded stuccowork – of this establishment would easily meet the standards of the famous French actress after whom this restaurant was named. Serves Czech and French cuisine. The Mucha menu includes a ticket to the eponymous museum.

5 **SALABKA**

K Bohnicím 2
Troja ⑩
+420 778 019 002
salabka.cz

This part of town, which is near the botanical garden, has a special holiday feel to it. The Salabka winery and restaurant offer fine dining among the vines. Take a stroll between courses and admire the amazing city views. On the weekend, Salabka serves a special seasonal tasting menu paired with their own wines. Reservations highly recommended.

5 places for a tasty
BREAKFAST OR BRUNCH

6 **CAFÉ LOUNGE**
Plaská 8
Lesser Town ③
+420 257 404 020
cafe-lounge.cz

Serving the best coffee in town for several years now, also the brunch menu in this elegant eatery is far from ordinary. Their backyard terrace borders on the Medieval Hunger Wall, which was allegedly commissioned by Charles II to create employment for the starving locals. Reservations highly recommended.

7 **BISTRO 34**
Újezd 34
Lesser Town ③
+420 775 779 548
bistro37.cz

In this bistro you can enjoy a juicy English breakfast or pancakes served from 7 am to 2 pm, surrounded by wild ducks and other fowl (the owner is a passionate hunter). Try to get there early before the hotel guests from upstairs flock in.

8 **MONOLOK CAFE**
Moravská 18
Vinohrady ④
+420 739 018 195
monolok.cz

Its sleek design contrasts with the lavish brunch menu. Eat your fill with their Croque Madame or fluffy pancakes and end your meal with a good coffee. When the day's first sunrays hit the courtyard terrace, the place is quite enchanting. Make sure you book in advance to secure a table.

9 **CAFÉ JEN**

Kodaňská 37
Vršovice ④
+420 604 329 904
cafejen.cz

Find this snug spot in the basement of a neo-Gothic building in the green Old Vršovice neighbourhood. Start your day in style with a full breakfast and mimosas. If you want to try their special weekend brunch menu, make a reservation to avoid a longish wait.

10 **TWENTY7**

Přístavní 27
Holešovice ⑧
+420 605 444 528
twenty7.cz

This part of town can be a little sleepy in the morning, but the busy bees in Phill's little bistro will already have your breakfast ready. Eat your full English, huevos rancheros or banana pancakes on the terrace or while you admire the nice black and white interior.

6 CAFÉ LOUNGE

The 5 best places to

EAT LIKE A LOCAL

11 **LOKÁL U BÍLÉ KUŽELKY**
Míšeňská 12
Lesser Town ③
+420 257 212 014
lokal-ubilekuzelky.ambi.cz

Choose the steak tartare on garlic-rubbed toast or a fat *talián* sausage with horseradish, like the local carnivores. Then wash it down with a frothy pint of pilsner on tap. But leave some room for dessert – *mlíko* is a rich, smooth and creamy pour, with plenty of sweet foam and just a bit of beer. Ticks the boxes for all the Czech classics.

12 **MINCOVNA**
Staroměstské náměstí 7
Old Town ①
+420 727 955 669
restauracemincovna.cz

As this is the only non-tourist-trap restaurant in Old Town Square, it can get very busy at lunchtime. You can't go wrong here whether you order the goulash, which is incredible every time, a sirloin steak or duck. The sleek, modern interior with wall decorations is a reminder that this place used to be a mint where coins were manufactured.

13 **U SLOVANSKÉ LÍPY**
Tachovské náměstí 6
Žižkov ⑤
+420 734 743 094
uslovanskelipy.cz

'Eat like a local' means 'eat a lot', so order the pork knuckle. Should one kilo of crunchy meat be too much, then treat yourself to a small beer snack, such as marinated cheese or pickled *gothaj* salami, as you sample one of the ten treasures they have on tap.

14 **U KROKA**
Vladislavova 12
Vyšehrad ②
+420 775 905 022
ukroka.cz

The legend of Count Krok and his three daughters started here at Vyšehrad. The locals come here for the excellent Pilsener beer and affordable lunches while the tables are populated with international guests in the evening. Their menu is available in five languages and includes most traditional Czech dishes.

15 **VINOHRADSKÝ PARLAMENT**
Korunní 1
Vinohrady ④
+420 224 250 403
vinohradskyparlament.cz

Even with its four large rooms this place always seems to be full to the rafters. Its modern decor combined with traditional cuisine was an immediate hit. The lunch menu changes with the seasons. Every Wednesday evening, they serve roast pork specials.

The 5 nicest restaurants

ON THE RIVER

16 **MATYLDA**
Masarykovo nábřeží
New Town ②
+420 724 800 100
botelmatylda.cz

Yes, they have an impressive Italian menu. But you will be unable to take your eyes off the splendour of this saloon ship. And once you do, there is always the Castle. Their selection of fresh fish and seafood and the water all around you will soon have you believe Prague has a coast.

17 **HERGETOVA CIHELNA**
Cihelná 2b
Lesser Town ③
+420 296 826 103
kampagroup.com/en/restaurants/hergetova-cihelna

A stylish restaurant with a spectacular view of the Charles Bridge. The restaurant's main dining room feels immense, an impression that is only enhanced by the many mirrors on the wall. Yet it somehow manages to retain an intimate ambience. Perfect for an evening tête-à-tête after a romantic walk on Kampa Island.

18 **MLÝNEC**
Novotného lávka 9
Old Town ①
+420 277 000 777
mlynec.cz

Chef Marek Šáda never stops looking for forgotten Bohemian specialities. His Czech tasting menu pairs his elegant cuisine with local seasonal ingredients. They serve fabulous brunches here, with the intrepid Vltava River underfoot. Book ahead and request a table in the far left corner.

19 MANÚ RISTO & LOUNGE

Dětský ostrov 25
Smíchov ⑦
+420 725 161 616
www.manuristo.cz

Emanuele Ridi has been a culinary celebrity since 2012, when he made his first appearance on Czech TV. His ristorante is located on a small islet near Vltava's left bank and serves Mediterranean cuisine and Italian wines. In the summer, the lounge is extended with an open-air pop-up bar.

20 PODOLKA

Podolské nábřeží - Přístav 1
Podolí ②
+420 774 115 166
podoli.restaurace podolka.cz

Make your way through the yacht club's car park into a modern wooden building. On the other side lies the largest bay of the Vltava River, making it a perfect mooring for motor and sailing boats. Unusually, half of the dishes on the menu are vegetarian. Take a digestive stroll along the port after your meal.

16 MATYLDA

The 5 best
BAKERIES

21 **PEKAŘSTVÍ KAMENICKÁ**
Kamenická 47
Bubeneč ⑧
+420 233 381 078
pekarstvi.cz

The tiny family bakery on the corner of this street has been supplying bread to the Czech Parliament for decades. Knock on the window or side door after your late-night pub crawl and who knows, you may well score some freshly-baked rolls straight from the oven.

22 **MANSSON'S BAKERY & CAFÉ**
Bílkova 6
Old Town ①
+420 222 310 620
mansson-bakery.com

This Czech-Danish family business has been supplying fancy hotels and restaurants since 1999. Their enterprise was so successful that they opened this cafe five years later. Choose between 100% rye bread, white Italian with olive oil or the Sarah Bernhardt chocolate cake, which is as divine as the famous French actress.

23 **PRAKTIKA BAKERY**
Bělehradská 66
Vinohrady ④
www.pekarnapraktika.cz

Here bread is baked with utter devotion to the artisanal, rural methods and traditions. You can choose between five types of loaf – spelt, rye, buckwheat, corn or polenta – and then argue which one is the best. The jury is still out.

24 ESKA

Pernerova 49
Karlín ⑥
+420 731 140 884
eska.ambi.cz

Eska only has two types of bread: the 33 and the 66. The difference: the proportion of rye flour in the three-stage sourdough. Their Italian oak wood oven ensures the impressively robust crust has a nice crunch to it. Before buying a rather pricy loaf, taste a slice topped with some homemade spread.

25 ANTONÍNOVO BAKERY

Moskevská 38
Vršovice ④
+420 733 593 925
antoninovopekarstvi.cz

The lights are on well before dawn to ensure the bread and crispy rolls are ready first thing in the morning. The sweet fragrance that wafts through the air will have you salivating in no time at all. Fortunately, they have a cafe that serves soup to go with the bread and coffee with the pastry.

5 *exceptional*
TRADITIONAL CAFES

26 **CAFÉ LOUVRE**
Národní 22
New Town②
+420 224 930 949
cafelouvre.cz

Take the middle entrance in bustling Národní Avenue, climb up two flights of stairs and see for yourself how little things have changed since the 1900s, when Franz Kafka or Albert Einstein used to spend 'pleasant and relaxing moments' here. It opens as early as 8 am and closes before midnight.

27 **CAFÉ SAVOY**
Vítězná 5
Smíchov ⑦
+420 257 311 562
cafesavoy.ambi.cz

A place in the grand European tradition, for breakfast or lunch. After it was taken over by a successful restaurant group, it is even closer to perfection. Treat yourself to a cake from their own patisserie, admire the listed neo-Renaissance stucco ceiling which has a high eye candy factor or enjoy the hustle and bustle while sipping a glass of wine.

28 **CAFÉ PLATÝZ**
Národní 37
Old Town ①
+420 224 211 161
cafeplatyz.cz

Hidden in a passage with the same name, this elegant cafe's interior combines bright geometric and floral patterns. It was designed by a famous film architect, in the style of the First Czechoslovak Republic.

27 CAFÉ SAVOY

29 KAVÁRNA OBECNÍ DŮM

AT: MUNICIPAL HOUSE

Náměstí republiky 5
Old Town ①
+420 222 002 763
kavarnaod.cz

Step inside and prepare yourself, because you will be overwhelmed. The stuccowork, the wood-panelled benches as well as the fountain at the farthest end are all one-hundred-year-old originals, while all but one chandelier are copies (ask your waiter which one). Czechoslovakia's independence was declared on the first floor of this establishment in 1918. One to remember.

30 CAFÉ IMPERIAL

Na Poříčí 15
New Town ①
+420 246 011 440
cafeimperial.cz

A classy Art Deco restaurant decorated with elaborate ceramic tiles and brocade blinds. The mastermind chef is Zdeněk Pohlreich, Gordon Ramsay's Czech counterpart, so expect an impeccable service and food. The lunch menu is very good value and they serve delicious homemade cakes.

27 CAFÉ SAVOY

5 *restaurants for*

MEAT LOVERS

31 **KANTÝNA**
Politických vězňů 5
New Town ①
kantyna.ambi.cz

You wouldn't expect to see marble and frescoes in a butcher's or a canteen, but Kantýna combines the two, with great effect! Choose a steak, a piece of roast, or a steak tartare, after which the waiter will jot it down on your little notepad. They charge by the weight here.

32 **BRIXTON BALLS**
Korunní 23
Vinohrady ④
+420 776 602 306
brixtonballs.cz

This tiny bistro serves a wide range of disarmingly good meat (as well as veggie) balls. Another story of someone who pursued his passion. One of the two owners is Tim Simenon, a record producer for David Bowie and Björk among others, who swapped beats for meatballs.

33 **LA BOTTEGA LINKA**
Havlíčkova 13
New Town ①
+420 222 314 961
bottegalinka.cz

This elegant eatery recently opened on the premises that had been vacated by Prague's most renowned delicatessen. They pride themselves on their XO-oven, an Italian invention for cooking fish or matured meats in special smoke at 480°C. It has earned quite the cult following, so book a table to be on the safe side.

34 **LA FINESTRA IN CUCINA**
Platnéřská 13
Old Town ①
+420 222 325 325
lafinestra.cz

Many superlatives have already been used for this cosy restaurant with its exposed brick interior and open kitchen, where you can see chef Tomáš Juřík at work. The menu is jam-packed with fresh authentic Italian delicacies. They claim to have the biggest selection of wines in town.

35 **DISH**
Římská 29
Vinohrady ④
+420 222 511 032
dish.cz

An excellent burger bistro that serves fabulous takes on classic dishes, unusual combinations of traditional (smelly!) Moravian cheese and caramelised onion with port wine, or savoury slow baked lamb. Choose what you want, but do eat it with their garlic and parsley bistro fries.

35 DISH

5

CLASSIC CZECH

dishes worth trying

36 **SMAŽENÝ SÝR**
SMUDGENEE SEER

Often the only vegetarian item on the menu. Under the breadcrumbs you'll often find deep-fried edam or hermelín cheese. As soon as it is placed before you on the table you have about 5 minutes to eat it, before it turns into a lump of rubbery cold cheese.

37 **NAKLÁDANÝ HERMELÍN**
NAKHLAADANEE HERMELEEN

This marinated camembert-wannabe should always be paired with beer. Cut in half and stuffed with garlic, herbs or nuts, it keeps for a few days (sometimes weeks), developing more and bigger flavours as time passes. Love it or hate it but at least give this legendary cheese a try.

38 **SVÍČKOVÁ**
SVEETCHKHOVAA

A delicious sirloin steak with a creamy vegetable sauce that has crossed the ocean all the way to Chicago (Czech ex-pats call it 'comfort food'). Don't be lazy. Make the short trip out of town to a village called Čakovičky - Na Pekárně to taste the best *svíčková* available.

39 **DRŠŤKOVÁ POLÉVKA**
DRSHKHOVAA POLEEVKA

This tripe soup is widely believed to be a hangover cure. No wonder it's so popular in Eastern Europe. The Czech version combines paprika, onions and garlic, imparting the soup with a very distinct spicy flavour. In fact, it's so delicious you might not even want to know it is made of cows' stomachs...

40 **CHLEBÍČEK**
KHLEBEETCHEK

A famous open-faced sandwich that recently celebrated its 100th anniversary. Designed to be wolfed down in a few bites, it consists of a slice of white bread with a rich mayonnaise spread, and a slice of cheese, ham, egg and a pickle. Taste it in a deli or during a break in the National Theatre with a glass of sekt.

40 CHLEBÍČEK

The 5 best
CHEAP EATS

41 **POLÉVKÁRNA**
Sokolovská 97
Karlín ⑥
+420 608 074 414

'All you need is soup', as any grandma from the Czech Republic – or Georgia – will tell you. In Polévkárna, these two traditions have been combined into a healthy menu which changes according to the seasons. One thing you'll definitely remember is the *khachapuri*, a Georgian bread with various fillings.

42 **SISTERS**
Dlouhá 39
Old Town ①
+420 775 991 975
chlebicky-praha.cz

'It is time for a little something...' said Winnie the Pooh and headed to Sisters for an open-faced sandwich. Here you will find *chlebíček* 4.0 – a sophisticated descendant of this traditional Czech dish, in healthier, vegetarian and (if you like) gluten-free varieties.

43 **KORUNKA U ARBESA**
Zubatého 2
Smíchov ⑦
+420 257 312 679

Opens at 7 am to allow blue collar workers to start their day with a bowl of hearty tripe (cow stomach) soup and beer. There are no seats in this authentic people's eatery: all the meals are consumed standing up. Expect no frills here. Try their traditional black pudding with cabbage or dill sauce and dumplings.

44 HOMELESS CHEFS

AT: JÍDELNA KUCHAŘEK BEZ DOMOVA

Brožíkova 6
Smíchov ⑦
+420 721 251 872

This vegan canteen is a social enterprise, which is staffed by women who used to be or still are homeless. After a couple of years in catering and operating a food truck, their dream of starting a proper bistro came true. A fantastic combination of healthy, affordable lunches with socially responsible consumption.

45 LAHOODKY

Komunardů 26
Holešovice ⑧
+420 605 324 914
lahoodky.cz

Faced with the globalisation in fast food, Filip Mičan's philosophy was to bring back the Czech tradition. This corner deli had been here for decades, but deserved a little make-over. Exposing the bricks and adding a sleek black-tiled backdrop did the trick. Throw all caution to the wind and pour your own Lobeč beer or Kofola from the tap.

44 HOMELESS CHEFS

5 *restaurants for a*
ROMANTIC DINNER

46 PÁLFFY PALACE

Valdštejnská 14
Lesser Town ③
+420 257 530 522
palffy.cz

You'll find a music academy in one of the shabby chic wings of this 18th-century Baroque palace. The restaurant is an altogether different cup of tea, with a flamboyant candle-lit dining room with mirrors on the walls, which serves Czech and French cuisine. On a budget? The three-course lunch menu is quite a bargain, and it helps that the food is quite delicious too.

47 CHATEAU LETNÁ

Letenské sady 341
Holešovice ⑧
+420 233 378 208
letenskyzamecek.cz

Prague's romantic souls have been dining on this hill for at least 150 years, since this Italian-style villa was built. Enjoy a game of pétanque, look for the oldest carousel in Europe, eat a sausage on the beer terrace or book the salon in the turret for a very special tête-à-tête, but make sure not to miss the sunset.

48 LUKA LU

Újezd 33
Lesser Town ③
+420 257 212 388
lukalu.cz

Run by the Djorem family, who are originally from Sarajevo, this is an incredibly authentic Balkan place. You'll feel as if you have just stepped onto a small street in Dubrovnik with shuttered windows on the walls and quirky lamps. Fish and seafood specials.

49 ZVONICE

Jindřišská věž
New Town ①
+420 224 220 009
restaurantzvonice.cz

A restaurant on the seventh floor of a gothic belfry that overlooks the rooftops of the New Town. While savouring their specialities do not forget to look up at the uncovered wooden beams and the Saint Mary bell cast in 1518. A bottle of Moravian wine will make the evening even more perfect.

50 MEZE

Karlínské náměstí 6
Karlín ⑥
+420 727 976 970
mezerestaurant.cz

'Sharing is caring', the concept behind this Mediterranean style restaurant which overlooks a pretty Karlín church. Prepare to enjoy a continuous flow of tasty hot and cold starters and dishes. The great wine list is an added bonus.

5 *of the best places for a*
HEALTHY LUNCH

51 **JINÁ KRAJINA**
Kodaňská 5
Vršovice ④
+420 271 742 541
kodanska.jinakrajina.cz

A restaurant that mainly serves vegetarian dishes made with fresh ingredients, some of them grown in their own greenhouse. Their lunch menu usually contains a vegetarian option and the prices here are more affordable than in the city centre.

52 **MEZI SRNKY**
Sázavská 19
Vinohrady ④
+420 732 238 833

The cafe's name roughly translates as 'Among the Deers' – a play on words dreamt up by the owners, who like to experiment with natural decorations. A trendy hangout with communal seating to promote interaction. The staff have good taste in music, speak good English, and serve excellent coffee and brunches.

53 **COBRA BAR**
Milady Horákové 8
Holešovice ⑧
+420 778 470 515
barcobra.cz

Only the paint on the walls offers a sense of this hip place's past life as a dodgy rave bar. Back then, there was no Asian-inspired lunch menu, no filling vegetarian soups or DJ lounge in the evenings. Fortunately, a group of friends got fed up with having to always make the trek downtown to enjoy this and opened Cobra Bar.

54 **CUKRKÁVALIMONÁDA**

54 **CUKRKÁVALIMONÁDA**
Lázeňská 7
Lesser Town ③
+420 257 225 396
cukrkavalimonada.com

Savour one of their salads under the 400-year-old wooden ceiling beams, then up your calorie intake with some homemade chocolates. Popular with an international crowd from the surrounding embassies and students of the Anglo-American University. Open all week for breakfast and lunch.

55 **BISTRO À TABLE!**
Mařákova 10
Dejvice ⑨
+420 211 152 619

A small French bistro near Hradčanská metro station, run by Jean-Charles Berger, who created an authentic Parisian corner here. The wide paved streets below and green trees above somehow helped him pull of this trick. Expect some seriously good French wines.

5 *restaurants with a* GREAT VIEW

56 **OBLACA**
Mahlerovy sady 1
Žižkov ⑤
+420 210 320 086
towerpark.cz

Fancy dining in the clouds? This restaurant is located 66 metres above the ground, in the TV tower with its iconic giant crawling babies. They have a good selection of meat dishes here and serve some chic seasonal menus, including veal and strawberry.

57 **BELLEVUE**
Smetanovo nábřeží 18
Old Town ①
+420 222 221 443
bellevuerestaurant.cz

This lavishly decorated corner building on the waterfront owes its name to its spectacular view of the Vltava and the Castle. Chef Petr Bureš likes to surprise his guests with his take on Czech cuisine, including grilled roe with roasted celery, chestnuts and cabbage, as well as excellent fish and seafood.

58 **CODA**
Tržiště 9
Lesser Town ③
+420 225 334 761
codarestaurant.cz

On this incredible rooftop terrace with a 360-degree view, chef David Šašek will tempt you with a Czech tasting menu that includes *Jihočeská kulajda* – a traditional sour cream, potato and mushroom soup. Most of the meats are prepared using the sous vide method.

59 TERRACE AT THE GOLDEN WELL

U Zlaté studně 4
Lesser Town ③
+420 257 533 322
terasauzlatestudne.cz

Indisputably the best view of the Lesser Town's rooftops and the Castle's palace gardens. That said, they serve an affordable lunch menu (2 courses for just 790 CZK). If it was fine for Obama and Michelle, it should be good enough for you too.

60 BASTION PRAGUE RESTAURANT

Horská 4
New Town ②
+420 736 114 124
bastion-prague.cz

Perched on the city fortifications this stylish restaurant, which overlooks the Nusle Valley and Vyšehrad fortress, is a real gem. The chefs prepare fancy tasting menus of three to seven courses, which are paired with some exquisite wines. The surrounding modern park is also an open air gallery.

59 TERRACE AT THE GOLDEN WELL

5 *of the nicest*

MODERN BISTROS

61 **BISTRO 8**
Veverkova 8
Holešovice ⑧
+420 730 511 973
www.bistro8.cz

This street has become a hype since the opening of Bistro 8. Go and try their lunch menu, which is inspired by all corners of the globe, or order a coffee with some non-milk – made of dates, almonds and a pinch of Himalaya salt.

62 **MARTIN'S BISTRO**
Velehradská 4
Vinohadry ⑤
+420 774 100 378

This laidback place feels like your local watering hole, where everybody is welcome (including kids and dogs). Martin puts together a carefully tailored menu (pairing food from around the world with French wines). A generous selection of spirits and cocktails is a reminder of his previous career as a bartender.

63 **KRYSTAL BISTRO**
Sokolovská 99
Karlín ⑥
+420 222 318 152
krystal-bistro.cz

Experienced chef Petr Tyrichtr decided to leave a famous gastro chain six years ago. His bistro aspires to continue the tradition of the simple Parisian eateries of the 1930s. Peek into the busy kitchen in the back room, a glass of Matuška IPA in hand.

64 BISTRO MILADA

Šmeralova 22
Bubeneč ⑧
+420 222 520 419

This is the closest you can get to a true French bistronomic experience in Prague. Treat yourself to three courses, each of them jam-packed with seasonal flavours and colours. If at some point you feel like licking their non-matching plates clean, then do – they will love you all the more for it! But make sure to save some room for their homemade marshmallows that come with the bill.

65 WINE FOOD MARKET

Strakonická 1
Smíchov ⑦
+420 733 338 650
winemarket.cz

This will be your shortest tram ride ever to Italy. Enter through the pasticceria, explore the flower stall, the fishmonger's and the pasta bar before sitting down at one of the long tables in the middle of the busy hall.

The 5 best

VEGETARIAN RESTAURANTS

66 **LEHKÁ HLAVA**
Boršov 2
Old Town ①
+420 222 220 665
lehkahlava.cz

You might struggle to find this restaurant on a street that is actually a courtyard. The initial effort pays off after which you will gladly trade in any steak in the world for their amazing grilled goat cheese with walnuts, spinach and a potato gratin. Book well in advance and ask for a table in the backroom 'under the stars'.

67 **MLSNÁ KAVKA**
Sokolovská 29
Karlín ⑥
+420 777 913 054
mlsnakavka.cz

Some say this social enterprise has the best vegetarian *nasi goreng* (Indonesian fried rice) in town. Run by a Dutch expat who married a prominent Czech feminist, Kavka's menu includes vegetarian, vegan and gluten-free dishes. On Sundays, they serve all you can eat brunch.

68 **MYRAW CAFÉ**
Gourmet Pasáž,
Dlouhá 39
Old Town ①
+420 603 889 016
myraw.cz

If raw vegan is your religion, then you might just need to close your eyes and nose to make it through the gourmet passage that leads to this cafe. Once there, you will be rewarded with a healthy daily lunch menu, delicious cakes and coffee served with nut milk.

69 **ETNOSVĚT**
Legerova 40
New Town ②
+420 226 203 880
etnosvet.cz

In this vibrant vegan bistro, an international team led by a French chef prepares a variety of dishes from around the world. Get ready for vegan pizzas, cucumber steak tartare or an entire tasting menu, all of which is served on beautiful plates. Lovely garden in the summer.

70 **ESTRELLA**
Opatovická 17
New Town ②
+420 777 431 344
estrellarestaurant.cz

On the ground floor with its green-shuttered windows they serve modern vegetarian cuisine in line with the latest international trends and Czech tradition. Refined, original and reasonably priced cooking. The attentive and friendly staff will make sure your visit is enjoyable.

66 LEHKÁ HLAVA

The 5 best

ASIAN RESTAURANTS

71 **MADAME LYN RESTAURANT**
Šafaříkova 18
Vinohrady ④
+420 606 307 777
madamelynrestaurant.cz

This family restaurant pays tribute to the long-standing Czech-Vietnamese special relationship. It has a simple interior but the oriental extravaganza starts on the menu: amazing bun cha (also in combo version), various types of pho, seafood skewers and French wine as a bonus, all reasonably priced.

72 **BAHN-MI-BA**
Jankovcova 8
Holešovice ⑧
+420 731 056 185
bahnmiba.cz

Their Vietnamese baguette sandwiches are a tasty reminder of the French colonial era. But the very first bite, topped with lemon grass and fresh coriander, will immediately make you forget about any uncomfortable historical consequences. Ask for extra chilli and wash it down with Tiger beer. Another branch downtown.

73 **MIYABI**
Navrátilova 10
New Town ②
+420 296 233 102
miyabi.cz

This place has been in business since 1995, serving delicious sushi, bentó boxes and monthly thematic menus. For a real experience, order a table in the backroom with floor seating on a *shakuhachi* evening.

74 **KABUL**
Krocínova 5
Old Town ①
+420 224 282 509
kabulrestaurant.cz

Afghan gourmet Hasib Saleh's cushy restaurant continues to be a venerable establishment even after it moved. Their lamb kebab skewers still come straight off the grill onto your plate, *ashak* dumplings filled with leek are still topped with kofta and mint yoghurt, and the *badonjane siah* eggplant dish still wows meat lovers.

75 **K THE TWO BROTHERS**
Petrská 12
New Town ①
+420 273 134 430
indian-restaurant-prague.com

As its name suggests, this place was opened by two Londoners of Indian origin. With crystal chandeliers, silver mirrors and large historic photos, the interior is somehow reminiscent of an Empire on which the sun never sets. Try their marvelous chicken *tikka masala*.

72 BAHN-MI-BA

The 5 best

ITALIAN RESTAURANTS

76 **AROMI**

Náměstí míru 6
Vinohrady ④
+420 222 713 222
www.aromi.lacollezione.cz

Located opposite the elegant Vinohrady Theatre, this classy restaurant is just as stylish as its neighbour. Its passionate owner, Riccardo Lucque, focuses on the simplicity of natural ingredients and organic products from small Italian growers and farmers. They have a wine list with about 300 Italian wines and over one hundred kinds of grappa.

77 **SAN CARLO**

Nosticova 1
Lesser Town ③
+420 257 312 518
sancarlo.cz

Napoletana pizza found its way to Prague via San Carlo. The kitchen entry is a confessional, with the inscription '*Ora et labora*' (pray and work). The vaulted walls are decorated with ornate floral patterns and combine beautifully with plush red velvet chairs and mirror mosaics to create an extravagant atmosphere. They have another branch in Dittrichova Street.

78 **PASTAŘ**

Malostranské nábřeží 1
Lesser Town ③
+420 777 009 108
pastar.cz

Pastař was founded when Jan Blažek, the founder of a Czech fresh pasta-making company, teamed up with his friend, Michelin-starred chef Tomáš Arnold. This authentic Italian family-style restaurant entices customers with a small deli counter in the store out front.

79 **OSTERIA DA CLARA**

Mexická 7
Vršovice ④
+420 271 726 548
daclara.com

A tiny Tuscan corner in Prague, with a simple unpretentious interior, that serves fragrant seafood and an excellent *Primitivo*. Their generous portions and homely atmosphere will make you come back again and again. Order the five-courses menu, which takes about three hours to eat.

80 **ICHNUSA BOTEGA BISTRO**

Plaská 5
Smíchov ⑦
+420 605 375 012
ichnusa.restaurant.cz

A real Sardinian retreat, a tiny place with just a few tables and no written menu (as it changes daily). Expect a family atmosphere and a warm welcome from the owner, Antonello Pranteddu. Only the best ingredients available are used here, paired with fragrant red wines and a glass of *myrto* at the end of your meal to promote digestion.

CAFÉ LETKA

75 PLACES FOR A DRINK

The 5 most

UNUSUAL PLACES TO HAVE A DRINK

81 **THE GRÉBOVKA VINEYARD PAVILION**

Havlíčkovy sady 1369
Vinohrady ④
+420 725 000 334

In the middle of a park that used to be a private garden of a rich industrial entrepreneur. The pavilion's first floor has a bar and gallery, the second floor is used to host private events. Local grapes are planted on a southern slope, making it one of the two places in Prague where wine is produced.

82 **CAFÉ VÍTKOV**

U Památníku 1900
Žižkov ⑤
+420 603 554 520
cafevitkov.cz

The equestrian statue of Vítkov Memorial is visible from everywhere in the city. Originally designed for the first Czechoslovak president, the monument honours the victory of the protestant Jan Žižka. Enjoy the scenic view from the cafe located on the 2nd floor of the gigantic building that once served as a mausoleum.

83 **CROSS CLUB**

Plynární 23
Holešovice ⑧
+420 736 535 010
crossclub.cz

Holešovice used to be an industrial district full of factories. With its industrial interior, Cross Club is a living witness. Ramble around the iron balconies, cog wheel mechanisms, chill on the outside terrace or dance all night long. Your call.

84 **(A)VOID**

Náplavka (under the railway bridge)
New Town ②
+420 602 211 181

A funky bar on a converted steam cargo boat. Its lower deck has a fireplace, a piano and swinging seats, the upper deck has a large terrace overlooking the old railway bridge on one side and the Castle on the other. It hosts electronic gigs every other day and occasional exhibitions.

85 **PÍSEK GATE/ PÍSECKÁ BRÁNA**

K Brusce 5
Hradčany ③
+420 233 321 313
piseckabrana.cz

Just a stone's throw from the castle, you will find the last surviving specimen of the city's Baroque ramparts in the city centre. Nowadays you can see an exhibition here or just have a drink. Once a month they organise a jazz concert.

The 5 best

WINE BARS

86 STRADA DEL VINO

Pštrossova 34
New Town ②
+420 777 448 289
strada-del-vino.cz

Taste by the glass or by the bottle. The wine list covers all Italian regions from Veneto to Puglia, but the owner, who will gladly share his know-how, clearly is in love with Tuscany. Try their Piadina or burrata with a good sprinkle of olive oil.

87 NA BŘEHU RHÔNY

Francouzská 84
Vršovice ④
+420 222 932 236
nabrehurhony.cz

After a few trips to Provence, Filip Hotový and Karel Karafiát made it their mission to promote wines from Côtes-du-Rhône. They based their concept on bag-in-box wines so customers can choose from a wide selection at affordable prices.

88 VELTLIN WINE BAR

Křižíkova 115
Karlín ⑥
+420 725 535 395
veltlin.cz

This bar was founded by a Czech-Polish poet called Bogdan Trojak. Every day they open different organic, natural biodynamic wines from all four corners of the former Habsburg Austrian-Hungarian Empire, i.e. from Northern Bohemia to Tuscany. Get ready for your most memorable Central European geography lesson.

89 **VINÁRNA NÁPLAVNÍ**
Náplavní 9
New Town ②
+420 241 416 546
vinarna-naplavni.cz

In 2012, an old taproom had to make way for this modern winery. The owner, Jiří Kalousek, invested his heart and soul into it, and the result is definitely worth it. They serve a good selection of Moravian and Hungarian wines from the barrel, starting at 14 CZK per 1 dcl.

90 **U ZELENÉHO MNICHA**
Jugoslávských partyzánů 34
Bubeneč ⑨
+420 776 085 899
uzelenehomnicha.cz

Take a seat around one of the wine barrel tables and start tasting South Moravian wines that cost less than 1 euro per glass. Venture into the deli next door (same owner) to decide whether Hungarian sausages or Dutch cheese will prevent you from getting too drunk.

88 VELTLIN WINE BAR

5 places to have GREAT COFFEE

91 **KÁVA**
Růžová 7
New Town ①
+420 604 340 291
kavaruzova.cz

Tucked away in a small street behind a church, this tiny place has just one and a half table inside, so locals get their favourite drug to go. You know the coffee will be good as soon as you inhale the aroma inside. Their káva roasted in one of Prague's suburbs is more than satisfying.

92 **BISTRO PROTI PROUDU**
Březinova 22
Karlín ⑥
+420 728 036 171
bistroprotiproudu.cz

'In coffee we trust' is the motto of this bistro, which serves breakfast all day. Designed as a tribute to František Křižík (the Czech Edison), who connected Karlín to Libeň with a tram line. The minimalistic clean lines of the interior contrast with the full-bodied coffees prepared by their barista.

93 **MÍSTO**
Bubenečská 12
Dejvice ⑨
+420 727 914 535
mistoprovas.cz

Dejvice needed a place like this, serving all-day breakfast on the weekend, as well as delicious cakes and coffee from an espressionistic coffee machine by Kees van der Western. A place to while away the day and totally worth the short wait that can occur in peak times.

94 **KOFÁRNA**
Zborovská 60
Smíchov ⑦
+420 737 454 962
kofarnakafe.cz

The smell of freshly roasted coffee greets you in the street. In the front, there is a small co-working space, at the back you can sit down in two bright rooms with some inspiring books. The staff take coffee very seriously, and the occasional wait is definitely worth it.

95 **MAMA COFFEE**
Londýnská 49
Vinohrady ④
+420 773 263 333
mamacoffee.cz

Everything started with a trip to South Ethiopia in 2007. Upon their return Marta and Daniel Kolský decided to launch their own coffee roasting company, making Mamma Coffee the oldest fair trade roastery in Central Europe. They now have seven cafes all over Prague, but this one, with its tiny front garden, was the very first one.

93 MÍSTO

5 quirky places to
DRINK WITH THE LOCALS

96 **KAVÁRNA KABINET**
Terronská 25
Bubeneč ⑨
+420 233 326 668

You might wonder why locals would want to spend their free time in a place that strongly resembles a science room full of stuffed birds, posters of plants and old globes. But then you try their waffles, hot chocolate or special beers and you know why. Because it is simply awesome.

97 **CAFE LETKA**
Letohradská 44
Holešovice ⑧
+420 777 444 035
cafeletka.cz

Open from 8 am, Letka attracts coffee addicts first thing in the morning. Around lunch young professionals start to flock in for their avocado sandwich. In the afternoon, it welcomes overwhelmed visitors from the neighbouring National Technical Museum. When darkness falls, the bar is a great place for an intimate date.

98 **ZÁZEMÍ**
Bartolomějská 13
Old Town ①
+420 776 693 326

Zázemí is a multicultural clubhouse, where you will end up bonding over drinks with the locals, and singing along with them. There is a (free) gig almost every night, and if you're up for it the piano in the big room awaits you. If need be, boost your courage with a few beers first.

99 DOBRÁ TRAFIKA

Korunní 42
Vinohrady ④
+420 737 907 635
dobratrafika.cz

This 18-year-old shop is a local institution. At first glance, it looks like an ordinary tobacco shop but follow the passage to get to the hidden cafe with its piano. In the morning the crowd usually consists of solitary newspaper readers and gossipy students; the evenings are for music performances.

100 ROH DRUŽSTEVNÍ KAVÁRNA

U Božích bojovníků 3
Žižkov ⑤
+420 608 729 071

A meeting place for environmentally minded people, run as a friends' cooperative. Order vegan sausages with a pint of their amazing beer and eat them by the burning stove. The staff are very friendly and speak good English. Open only in the afternoon except on Tuesdays and Wednesdays.

5 *bars with a*
LONG BEER LIST

101 **BASE CAMP**
U Sudánky 27
Bubeneč ⑧
+420 773 260 707
pifko.info

Descend into a small cellar with a few tables, many crates and walls lined with beer fridges or shelves. This is a self-service bar and their selection is daunting so don't be tempted to taste all the beers they have. People have tried and failed, even crawling back up the stairs.

102 **BRUXX**
Náměstí Míru 9
Vinohrady ④
+420 224 250 404
bruxx.cz

Let's be clear. Czech beer is great. But Belgian brews are still more complex and varied. This Brussels style brasserie has a good selection of hoppy gems, although the fries are nowhere near as crispy as the ones you would get from a Belgian *fritkot*. Popular with families because of the large kids play area.

103 **ZUBATÝ PES**
K Botiči 2
Vršovice ④
+420 775 638 737
zubatypes.cz

Hop on the tram to visit the Toothy Dog. They usually have sixteen beers on tap, half of which are foreign. The owner is a passionate knowledgeable beer connoisseur, who speaks good Russian and some English. Fight for a seat at the bar.

104 **ZLÝ ČASY**
Čestmírova 5
Nusle ④
+420 723 339 995
zlycasy.eu

'Good drinks will make you forget bad times' is the mantra here and the locals seem to think this is a good place to achieve a state of amnesia. With up to twenty beers on tap at a time this little dungeon even inspires them to write odes to beer. It gets very busy, so better book ahead.

105 **PIVOVARSKÝ KLUB**
Křižíkova 17
Karlín ⑥
+420 222 315 777
pivovarskyklub.com

Here is where all the best brewers come for their Prague meeting. Enter through the store and follow the winding staircase up to the bar, where you can choose from 250 bottled and 6 draft beers. Most are Czech, but occasionally a guest from Germany, Belgium or Denmark drops by.

105 PIVOVARSKÝ KLUB

The 5 most

STYLISH AND HIP(STER) CAFES

106 **LA BOHEME CAFÉ**
Sázavská 32
Vinohrady ④
+420 734 207 049
labohemecafe.eu

The American Charles Fleer first shook hands with a coffee farmer in 2003. He has been travelling to plantations all around the world since. Come and join an international hip crowd as they sip their flat whites and fritz kolas. Wi-Fi is a treat reserved for those who order one drink every hour.

107 **KAVÁRNA CO HLEDÁ JMÉNO**
Stroupežnického 10
Smíchov ⑦
+420 775 466 330
kavarnacohledajmeno.cz

An unexpected trendy gem is hidden in this dodgy courtyard behind a car park. In the summer sit outside, on a pile of firewood, and gaze at the stars as you reflect on the colourful past life of the shabby bar van.

108 **URBAN CAFÉ**
Na Poříčí 37
New Town ①
cafeurban.cz

Housed in a building that trained 600 members of the WWII resistance. Half of the cafe is a garden, with one wall completely covered with potted plants. Take a seat at one of the shared tables and enjoy your cup of coffee, which is roasted by Berlin-based Fjord.

109 EMA ESPRESSO BAR

Na Florenci 3
New Town ①
+420 730 156 933
emaespressobar.cz

Are you willing to compromise on comfort for good coffee? Conveniently located near a busy train station, this place is often packed. You might end up sipping your V Drip while sitting on the stairs, but if you are looking for the perfect spot for some people watching, you've found it.

110 SUPER TRAMP COFFEE

Opatovická 18/Spálená 15
New Town ②
+420 777 446 022
supertrampcoffee.cz

A hidden passage connecting Opatovická and Spálená Streets leads to a small courtyard. The passage was rundown for many years but recently a quiet cafe serving great coffee, cakes and homemade goodies opened here. Try cascara – the invigorating infusion of cherries aka the poor man's coffee.

107 KAVÁRNA CO HLEDÁ JMÉNO

5 great places for
JAZZ AND BLUES

111 **JAZZ DOCK**
Janáčkovo nábřeží 2
Smíchov ⑦
+420 774 058 838
jazzdock.cz

It would be hard to find a more relaxing music bar in Prague. This is the only place you can listen to the soothing sound of jazz surrounded by the river. Its acoustic setup means this bar can play music until early morning, with two different concerts every night. Absolutely delightful.

112 **MALOSTRANSKÁ BESEDA**
Malostranské náměstí 21
Lesser Town ③
+420 257 409 123
malostranska-beseda.cz

This former town hall of the Lesser Town (Malá Strana in Czech) has played an important role in the cultural and political emancipation of the Czech nation. The first floor club hosts jazz and blues, as well as folk, chanson and bluegrass concerts.

113 **JAZZ REPUBLIC**
Jilská 1a
Old Town ①
+420 221 183 552
jazzrepublic.cz

Located in the heart of the Old Town, just a 4-minutes walk from Národní metro station. This place hosts a different type of gig every night, always starting at 9.15 pm (doors open at 8 pm). They serve a light dinner, such as tapas, sandwiches or cheeses to keep guests from starving.

114 KAŠTAN - SCÉNA UNIJAZZU

Bělohorská 150
Břevnov ③
+420 233 353 020
kastan.unijazz.cz

In 1878, this old inn witnessed the foundation of the Czech workers' movement. Nowadays it is a local community and cultural centre. They created the so-called Popmuseum, a nostalgic exhibition of musical instruments, including Czech-made electric guitars and keyboard instruments that were played in former Czechoslovakia. The adjacent Únik Café has a lovely terrace.

115 CLUB BLUES BAHNHOF

Mlýnská 2a
Bubeneč ⑨
+420 776 568 710
bluesbahnhof.com

Even if your train passed by slowly enough, you would still hardly pay attention to the building opposite what used to be Bubeneč train station. With its run-down façade and wild garden it looks more like a hermit's abode than a private blues club serving a fine selection of French wine and whisky.

5 of the coolest
OPEN AIR BARS

116 **NA HRADBÁCH**
V Pevnosti 2
Vyšehrad ②
+420 734 112 214
praha-vysehrad.cz

You have earned your drink after climbing up all the stairs to Vyšehrad Fortress. Once there, make your way through Leopold Gate and on your left you will spot this *hospůdka* (little pub), which serves good lager and Balkan grilled specialities. Now just wait for the sunset while savouring your *pljeskavica*.

117 **CAFÉ ŠESTÁK**
Vítězné náměstí
Dejvice ⑨

Thanks to some enterprising Czechs, this dead-end street car park was transformed into a lovely cafe with a bar truck. The programme features concerts, piano jams, creative workshops or free dance lessons. Ball and board games will keep you busy in between events.

118 **LETNÁ BEER GARDENS**
Letenské sady
Holešovice ⑧
+420 724 170 940

Come sit on Letná hill, in the shade of massive horse chestnut trees. After the climb, you can quench your thirst with a chilled beer or a draft Kofola at very affordable prices and enjoy the panoramic view of the city centre with the most spectacular sunsets.

119 NÁPLAVKA

Rašínovo nábřeží
New Town ②
prazskenaplavky.cz

Prague only recently realised the immense potential of its river banks. First, bars started to pop up, followed soon after by boats, water adventure facilities and even a floating beach volleyball pitch. Náplavka captures the mood of the summer season with cultural events and festivals in this 500-metre-long bar, which is open from April till October.

120 TISKÁRNA NA VZDUCHU

Areál Výstaviště 67
Holešovice ⑧
+420 602 679 625
tiskarnanavzduchu.cz

Find this little gem on the edge of Stromovka Park and the Expo grounds. Open from the early afternoon. A great place where culture, fun and current affairs come together. Check their programme to see when the next DJ set, swing dance-party or cinema screening will be held.

119 NÁPLAVKA

The 5 nicest

GAY-FRIENDLY BARS

121 **Q CAFÉ**

Opatovická 12
New Town ②
+420 776 856 361
q-cafe.cz

Tucked away in a small street near the river, Q Café is a cool hangout for people inside and outside of the queer community. Friendly staff mix good cocktails and the atmosphere is always very welcoming. If you are looking to score a hot date, sit near the bar. Head downstairs for a quiet chat.

122 **CLUB TERMIX**

Třebízského 4a
Vinohrady ④
+420 222 710 462
www.club-termix.cz

Ring the bell at the steel gate to be admitted to this private gay club with a pink Fiat parked in one of its walls. It opens just a few nights every week and is always very lively, but Wednesdays are most popular because of the Czech golden hits night. No cover and reasonable prices.

123 **CAFÉ & BAR SAPFÓ**

Slezská 74
Vinohrady ④
+420 720 297 420
sapfo.cz

Sappho was a Greek female poet, born on the Isle of Lesbos, and the inspiration for Petra and Alice's lesbian refuge in the heart of this gay neighbourhood. Open only in the evening with frequent concerts and DJ parties.

124 **SAINTS BAR**

Polská 32
Vinohrady ④
+420 222 250 326
praguesaints.cz

This long-standing British-run LGBT bar attracts an English-speaking international crowd. They will be happy to provide some insider tips about the Prague gay scene. An intimate bar that regularly hosts events, including the infamous quiz on the last Sunday of each month.

125 **CAFÉ CAFÉ**

Rytířská 10
Old Town ①
+420 224 210 597
www.cafe-cafe.cz

A great meeting point in the city centre with delicious cakes, breakfast until noon and light meals and salads. Very popular with Prague's fashion community, who love to see and be seen here. If you feel that your hipster factor is lacking, then look at the flatscreen TVs for some inspiration as they broadcast fashion channels non-stop.

5

ARTY AND LITERARY CAFES

126 MLÝNSKÁ KAVÁRNA

Všehrdova 14
Lesser Town ③
+420 257 313 222

You enter from the park on Kampa Island, over a little bridge that spans across Čertovka canal, right next to the wooden mill wheel. This is where the liberal elite, politicians and artists gather. You are very likely to bump into the sculptor David Černý or a former minister here.

127 LEICA GALLERY PRAGUE

Školská 28
New Town ②
+420 222 211 567
lgp.cz

The double-height ceilings of this elegant cafe make it a perfect venue for photo exhibitions. There are always some beautiful pictures in the back room (pay to enter). They only serve quality Czech wine from Kubík winery and French wines by Gayda.

128 LITERÁRNÍ KAVÁRNA ŘETĚZOVÁ

Řetězová 10
Old Town ①
+420 222 220 681
kavarnaretezova.cz

An incredibly peaceful place in a quiet street just off the main tourist route, with excellent Sardinian wine by the glass and savoury snacks. In the cellar they regularly host book launches, blues concerts, debates on current issues or literary festivals. Bliss.

129 **KAVÁRNA LIBERÁL**
Heřmanova 6
Holešovice ⑧
+420 732 355 445

An extremely laidback cafe belonging to a seasoned traveller and dandy called Jakub Štorek. Its authentic old-fashioned atmosphere attracts intellectuals who exchange views over a freshly tapped pint of Únětické. They serve decent wine by the glass and one or two tasty meals every day (pray that they're serving their goulash).

130 **KAVÁRNA POTRVÁ**
Srbská 2
Dejvice ⑨
+420 222 963 707
potrva.cz

It all started with a bunch of amateur theatre actors who needed a space to stage their plays. Over time, it developed into a project in a cosy basement with a cafe and a theatre. The cafe welcomes cool new bands, theatre performances, movie screenings and talks ten times a month.

126 MLÝNSKÁ KAVÁRNA

5 *chic*

COCKTAIL BARS

131 **L'FLEUR**
V Kolkovně 5
Old Town ①
+420 734 255 665
lfleur.cz

Around the corner from the upmarket shopping street, L'Fleur takes pride in having the largest collection of champagne in the country, comprising over 200 varieties. The ideal place to test the validity of the claim that drinking champagne in any quantity will never end with a visit to hangoverville.

132 **HEMINGWAY BAR**
Karolíny Světlé 26
Old Town ①
+420 773 974 764
hemingwaybar.eu

The art of mixology at its finest. Come here to impress or be impressed. This bar devotes a lot of attention to the favourite drinks of its namesake, namely absinthe, rum and champagne. To broaden your horizons, pre-order a rum tasting experience. Check out the antique cash register before leaving.

133 **VLKOVA 26**
Vlkova 26
Žižkov ⑤

One of the classier bars in Žižkov, in a street just above the Bohemians' football stadium, attracting a hip young crowd with its live (often female) DJ sets. On Sunday mornings, they organise popular pizza brunches.

134 PARLOUR

Krakovská 15
New Town ②
+420 777 200 015
parlour.cz

There are no menus here. Just tell the bartender how you feel and they will transform your mood into a personalised cocktail. Get a seat at the bar to watch the magic happen or sit under the vaulted ceilings and inspect the murals.

135 BLACK ANGEL'S BAR

Staroměstské náměstí 29
Old Town ①
+420 224 213 807
blackangelsbar.cz

Tucked in a gothic cellar in the main square this bar's interior is simply mesmerising. The menu skilfully imitates the diary of Alois Krcha, who allegedly developed all their recipes. Each cocktail is tied to his personal story, making for a witty and fun read. Even more fun to drink though.

132 HEMINGWAY BAR

5 places with a GREAT TERRACE

136 **ALYCHYMISTA**
Jana Zajíce 7
Bubeneč ⑧
+420 732 938 046
www.alchymista.cz

This tearoom, next to the coffee museum, has been serving its delicious cakes to locals since 1998. They also have a lovely garden with a fishpond. Treat yourself to a slice of cheesecake under a rosebush and try to make friends with the local black cat called Howard.

137 **KAVÁRNA ČEKÁRNA**
Vratislavova 8
Vyšehrad ②
+420 601 593 741
kavarnacekarna.cz

A genius creation of a garden, divided into two levels by a vaulted brick structure. The upper level belongs to the Reformist church (together with the building), the lower to thirst-quenching cafe goers. Try their yummy coffee during the day or Moucha beer with some pickled cheese in the evening.

138 **CAFÉ PAVLAČ**
Víta Nejedlého 23
Žižkov ⑤
+420 222 721 731
cafepavlac.cz

This family cafe has a quaint backyard with potted plants, an ivy-covered wall and typical Žižkov galleries overhead. They serve hearty breakfasts, daily lunch menus, light suppers, homemade desserts and lemonades made from fresh fruit. Ticks all the perfect cafe boxes.

139 **STYL & INTERIER**

Vodičkova 35
New Town ②
+420 222 543 128
stylainterier.cz

This house with its Baroque portal is striking because it is so small compared with the surrounding buildings. A short passage that serves as a showroom will take you to a courtyard with Gothic vaults, that dates back to the times of Charles IV. Sit down in one of their colonial-style chairs and order anything you feel like.

140 **BISTRO ZAHRADA**

Belgická 33
Vinohrady ④
+420 734 266 315
bistro-zahrada.cz

The concept of this place evolves around their back garden, with its large terrace, herb rockery and a vegetable patch. They are open all day serving breakfast, lunch and dinner, as well as brunch on the weekends, paired with excellent coffee and wine. A real urban delight.

The 5 best

SMALL BREWERIES

141 **KLÁŠTERNÍ ŠENK**

Markétská 1
Břevnov ③
+420 220 406 294
klasternisenk.cz

At Saint Vojtěch monastery, monks have been brewing beer for several centuries, more precisely since 993. They specialise in (dark) lagers, a stout, an IPA and a wheat beer. The adjacent taproom gets quite busy at weekends so better book ahead.

142 **BREWERY U DOBŘENSKÝCH**

U Dobřenských 3
Old Town ①
+420 222 222 141
pivovarudobrenskych.cz

Possibly Prague's smallest brewery covering a floor area of 14 sqm and a 400 litre copper. They specialise in herbal beers. Their main specialities include a tribulus ale and a salvia stout. Other types (such as mint, lemon balm, elderberry or buckthorn) are seasonal. The cosy interior with its fireplace and friendly staff are a winning combo.

143 **KOLČAVKA BREWERY**

Nad Kolčavkou 8
Libeň ⑧
+420 736 735 685
pivovarkolcavka.cz

After 86 years, the old beer-brewing tradition was revived in Libeň. The only Prague beer made by a female brewer. A 500-pound copper stands in the middle of the restaurant, so visitors can witness the brewing process.

144 **MINIBREWERY BEZNOSKA PROSEK**

Klíčovská 11
Prosek ⑧
+420 286 583 299
skolicka.cz

Quite far out of the city centre, but certainly worth the short metro ride. Occupying a building of a former elementary school, this brewery likes to experiment with lager, stout or ale, made on the spot in small quantities. If you overdo it on the tasting, there is always a B&B on the first floor.

145 **VINOHRADSKÝ BREWERY**

Korunní 106
Vinohrady ④
+420 222 760 080
vinohradskypivovar.cz

Half of the large vaulted cellars are used for the brewing, fermentation and aging of several beer types – traditional unfiltered lagers made with Czech malt and hops, as well as increasingly popular specials. The other half, which is connected by round windows, is home to a pub, a restaurant and an underground club.

The 5 best
BEERS TO TRY

146 **SVATÝ NORBERT IPA**

This is a non-filtered Indian Pale Ale from Strahov Monastery. Traditionally brewed for long distance transport to India, IPA now inspires European brewmasters to create bitter lagers. This one is a top-fermented beer, combining a full malt body with a lot of bitterness and a hoppy aroma.

147 **MATUŠKA PŠENIČNÉ**

This Bavarian-style Hefeweizen (wheat beer) is quite crisp, bready, with a healthy dose of yeast. Best enjoyed in a traditional slim, tall, curved glasses. Wheat beers are among the oldest beer styles, dating back to the Middle Ages, and enjoying a renaissance these days.

148 **CLOCK 12° AMERICAN PALE ALE**

Unfiltered light lager of gold colour and lower dense foam. It has an aroma of refreshing citrus and earthy hops, a medium-sized malted body with balanced bitterness, but the distinctive character of American hops by Simcoe and Cascade.

149 **NOMÁD EASY RIDER**

As its name suggests, Nomád is a gipsy brand without its own brewery. They travel around the world to draw inspiration and then contract out their recipes to better equipped partners. Easy Rider is their main beer, a dry American Pale Ale.

150 **ÚNĚTICE**

This small town, to the east of Prague, has been brewing beer for centuries. They have two flagship lagers: 10° is a hoppy light beer with lower alcohol content, while 12° has a stronger yeast fragrance, golden colour and mild yeast turbidity.

147 MATUŠKA PŠENIČNÉ

5 of the most classy
HOTEL BARS

151 **CAFÉ PALACE**
AT: HOTEL PALACE
Panská 12
New Town ①
+420 224 093 163
palacehotel.cz/en/dining

The Art Nouveau Palace Hotel opened here in 1909 and there has been a cafe on the ground floor of this majestic building ever since. Autographed photos of famous guests including Jacqueline Kennedy and Pink Floyd line the deep red walls. Affordable lunch menu served on weekdays.

152 **PIANO BAR**
AT: HOTEL PRESIDENT
Náměstí Curieových 100
Old Town ①
+420 234 614 100
hotelpresident.cz/gastronomy/piano-bar

This hotel, which was built on the right river bank in 1985, may not be the most picturesque in Prague, which is why the management is working hard on its reconstruction. On the ground floor mezzanine you will find the Piano Bar, with a glamorous contemporary interior, a fireplace wall and live music.

153 **PENTAHOTEL PRAGUE**
Sokolovská 112
Karlín ⑥
+420 222 332 800
pentahotels.com

Dim purple lighting, snug leather sofas and the possibility to rent a snooker table make the Penta hotel bar a welcome retreat for an intimate meeting or an after-work hangout.

154 **BAROCCO VENEZIANO CAFÉ**
AT: ALCHYMIST GRAND HOTEL
Tržiště 19
Lesser Town ③
+420 257 286 011
alchymisthotel.com/en/cafe-prague

The name pretty much sums it up – expect a Venetian-inspired, richly decorated interior with gilded stuccos, mirrors and period paintings. Have one of their homemade chocolates or cakes and enjoy the lovely view over the Lesser Town's rooftops.

155 **TOWER LOUNGE BAR**
AT: NH PRAGUE CITY HOTEL
Mozartova 1
Smíchov ⑦
+420 257 153 111
nh-hotels.com/hotel/nh-prague-city

Walk past the lobby cafe to reach the lift on your right. Upon entry, you will realise it is actually a cable car that will take you 50 metres up to the hilltop part of the hotel. On its 4th floor sits a bar offering splendid city views. A drink or two always makes the trip more memorable.

154 BAROCCO VENEZIANO CAFÉ

LUCIELA TASCHEN

70 PLACES TO SHOP

5 trendy
WOMEN'S FASHION STORES

156 **LEEDA**
Bartolomějská 1
Old Town ①
+420 775 601 185
leeda.cz

One of the oldest fashion brands on the block, with a contemporary look and feel. It has evolved a lot since its establishment in 2003 by two designers, who are both called Lucie. The place to go for flairy, feminine dresses in soft shades, as well as some flashy casualwear and accessories and jewellery by local designers.

157 **BACKYARD**
V Jirchářích 8
New Town ②
+420 605 894 096
back-yard.cz

You guessed it right, this place is tucked away in a cosy nook, which you can only access through a short green passage. Eight designers take turns managing the shop in between creative sessions in the studios on the first floor. If there is no fashion show when you drop by, then have a chat with them over a glass of wine or coffee.

158 **LA GALLERY NOVESTA**
Elišky Krásnohorské 9
Old Town ①
+420 734 574 868
lagallery.cz

A multi-brand shop created in support of Czech and Slovak designers. It provides a platform for young clothing and jewellery designers who do not have their own sales outlet yet. The selection changes regularly, with around three dozen brands presented at the same time.

159 **TINA HOLLAS COUTURE**
U Obecního dvora 4
Old Town ①
+420 602 325 125
tinahollas.com

Tiny Tina has been tailoring pretty clothes since 1996, and in the last three years, has been operating from this showroom and atelier rolled into one. Her casually elegant pieces are made of comfortable organic cotton, cashmere and silk, all in natural shades that are mostly of Italian origin.

160 **LUCIELA TASCHEN**
Petrská 10
New Town ①
+420 777 873 447
lucielataschen.com

A Czech brand of handmade leather bags, each of them lovingly produced by local craftsmen using as many local resources as possible. The most recent line was LT REDESIGN featuring the Míla model – an old bag from the 1980s which was transformed into a new one using local vegetable tanned leather in a wide range of colours.

5 original MEN'S FASHION STORES

161 **TONAK**
Žatecká 14
Old Town ①
+420 734 519 959
tonak.cz

Tonak has specialised in the manufacture of woollen and fur felt hats since 1799. Take your pick from berets, fezzes, caps and bowler hats. The traditional headwear called *zmijovka* makes a great souvenir and is perfect for chilly or windy weather. Its name refers to the viper-like pattern.

162 **THE ROOM BY BASMATEE**
Školská 7
New Town ②
+420 222 967 770
basmatee.cz

Tucked away in a small street not far from busy Wenceslas Square, this boutique offers a particularly well curated selection of streetwear and casual clothes. Brands they sell include Maharishi (UK), Gosha Rubchinkiy (Russia) (including the perfumes), Moma shoes (from Italy)... At the upper end of the price range.

163 **SEGRASEGRA**
Urxova 6
Karlín ⑥
segrasegra.com

Two sisters launched this fashion brand in 2007 to free bikers from multicoloured sportswear, developing fashionable yet functional gear for urban cyclists instead. Fancy a bicycle tire belt or a full cycling suit? Then you've come to the right place.

164 BOHEMPIA

Sokolovská 76
Karlín (6)
+420 773 475 625
bohempia.eu

Promotes and sells Bohemian-made hemp products, including shoes, clothes, underwear, textiles, linen and salves. What sets apart their simple styles and colours are the antimicrobial, antiseptic and thermos-regulating characteristics of natural hemp fibre. The perfect choice for environment-aware customers who are looking for sustainable slow fashion.

165 KRISPOL STORE

Ladova 5
New Town (2)
+420 731 203 720
krispolstore.cz

The very first store in Prague to specialise in bow ties with original patterns made of local fabrics and materials. The owner's ambition was to restore this forgotten accessory to its rightful place on men's necks again. It proved an immediate hit with the city's hip crowd. With every purchase, you also get a crash course on how to tie your new bow tie.

161 TONAK

The 5 most interesting places for VINTAGE SHOPPING

166 **BOTAS 66**
Křížkovského 18
Žižkov ⑤
+420 223 012 991
botas66.com

The outcome of a student art project based on the iconic Botas Classic model. It was launched in Czechoslovakia in 1966 and led to the inclusion of the word *botasky* in Czech vocabulary to refer to any sport shoe. Funky colours and the shape of running shoes combine to make super special one of a kind sneakers.

167 **BOHO**
Francouzská 76
Vršovice ④
+420 733 206 929
boho.cz

Like a true Bohemian couple Patrik and Patricia met in London. Back in Prague they set up this multifunctional space as their second home, selling an eclectic mix of vintage and retro fashion. Admire Patricia's DIY creations ranging from jewellery to candles and furniture. Then visit Patrik's Boho Café in Ondříčkova 8.

168 **GALERIE 22**
Husitská 22
Žižkov ⑤
+420 222 717 633
galerie22.cz

An exhibition space that also sells unique pieces of Bauhaus, Art Deco and Functionalist furniture, sourced from France and the Czech Republic. Each piece is carefully restored in their specialised atelier on the first floor of the same building.

169 PÁTÝ ELEMENT

Veverkova 28
Holešovice ⑧

A secondhand shop selling various theatre and folk costumes, an ideal place for bold and eccentric fashionistas. For some reason, they also have an extensive collection of male and female Tyrolian shirts, which may inspire a new trend in the years to come.

170 ANTIQUE AHASVER

Prokopská 3
Lesser Town ③
+420 257 531 404
ahasver.com

Entering this store is like climbing into your grandmother's closet. They sell every imaginable object from folk costumes, accessories and wedding dresses to bed linens, tea sets and Christmas decorations. Regardless of whether you are looking for something fancy or a collector's item, this is the perfect place to immerse yourself in the world of yesteryear.

167 BOHO

5 *unique*

CONCEPT STORES

171 **INGREDIENTS**
Jáchymova 2
Old Town ①
+420 224 239 477
ingredients-store.cz

A joint project of Jakub Kopčák and Lukáš Loskot aims to bring unconventional brands to the Czech market. Their range of perfumes and fragrance candles is supplemented by an assortment of natural paints and decorative cosmetics. But everything they sell has one thing in common: all the ingredients are of outstanding quality.

172 **BISTRO NO. 19**
Karolíny Světlé 19
Old Town ①
+420 776 797 242
no19.cz

This shop sells the best design accessories by Czech and international designers. They all have in common that they are used for food preparation and dining. A small bistro and gallery serve as a meeting place for high-quality food, design, art and the people who make, like and use it.

173 **CIHELNA**
Cihelná 2b
Lesser Town ③
+420 257 317 318
cihelnaprague.com

A concept design store with a curatorial selection of the best contemporary Czech glass, porcelain, jewellery, lights, objects and furniture. Over 60 sellers take turns running the space in this unique building, which used to be a part of a brickworks.

174 **SMETANAQ**

Smetanovo nábřeží 4
Old Town ①
smetanaq.cz

A building that received nation-wide media coverage in 2013 after a large gas explosion. It recently reopened its doors to designers of handmade fashion and jewellery. They can rent out studios, sell their creations in a design store and welcome their customers in the trendy groundfloor cafe.

175 **VNITROBLOCK**

Tusarova 31
Holešovice ⑧
+420 770 101 231

Covering a floor area of 2000 sq m, this is surely the largest concept store in town selling sustainable fashion and interior design. They host live DJ sets, art exhibitions, DIY workshops or interesting lectures here every week. There is a small cinema in the cellar, a cafe that serves great coffee on the groundfloor and a dance school, on the first floor.

174 **SMETANAQ**

5 stylish

DESIGN SHOPS

176 **MODERNISTA**
AT: VINOHRADSKY PAVILON
Vinohradská 50
Vinohrady ④
pavilon.cz

First a mill and factory, then a market hall and now a temple of design furniture with a dozen of different brands. Check Modernista offering the best Czech design of the last century, from cubist chandeliers to Adolf Loos's favourite couch or famous wooden toys. Free art gallery in the cellar.

177 **HOLPORT**
Komunardů 32
Holešovice ⑧
+420 266 199 452
holport.com

This immense showroom in a former factory is easy to find thanks to the tall brick chimney that bears its name. Two floors are dedicated to Konsepti furniture, you can find Artemide lights in the attic, while DesignSchool promotes interior design education.

178 **PAPELOTE**
Vojtěšská 9
New Town ②
+420 774 719 113
papelote.cz

Denisa Šachová's graduation project came to life here in 2010. She presents original handmade notebooks and stationery from recycled, and high-quality non-bleached Norwegian paper. Their *carta* collection will instantly make you feel the urge to write a letter, to anyone really.

179 HARDDECORE GALLERY

Senovážné náměstí 10
New Town ①
+420 775 417 230
harddecore.cz

This joint showroom presents the work of Josefína and Petr Bakoš, a couple who search for inspiration worldwide. She is a gifted fashion designer, while he is interested in anything from jewellery to bird feeders, as long as they are sustainably produced. You can visit their studio on the third floor.

180 LAVMI

Zlatnická 12
New Town ①
+420 230 234 974
lavmi.com

Lavmi finds itself at the intersection of art and interior design, selling vibrant and bright vlies wallpapers, textiles with geometric shapes and photos, or playful clocks. It is the shared project of life partners Babeta Ondrová and Jan Slovák. Their mountainous murals for adults or funky animals for children are full of creative energy and will add a blast of colour to your daily life.

176 MODERNISTA

5 *inspiring*

BOOKSHOPS

181 BAOBAB

Krymská 29
Vršovice ④
xaoxax.cz

The flagship store of a publishing house specialising in picture books, contemporary illustration and comic strips, including some experimental projects with very small print runs. The cosy venue is frequently transformed into a gallery, workshops for children, or a reading room for book launches. No children yet? No worries, they welcome all youthful souls.

182 K-A-V-K-A

Krocínova 5
Old Town ①
+420 606 030 202
kavkaartbooks.com

This elegant bookstore near the National Theatre specialises in fine arts and photography. It has a small foreign language section, but many other volumes are bilingual. They also sell the works of living Czech artists, who like to drop in when they are downtown.

183 AURORA

Spálená 53
New Town ②
+420 222 362 756
eaurora.cz

This secondhand store sells books, records, CDs and maps, new items arrive every day. They have a decent foreign language section on the first floor. If you prefer the smell of new books, head to the front store giving into the street.

184 PAGEFIVE

Veverkova 5
Holešovice ⑧
+420 774 262 553
pagefive.com

This independent store, which won the Czech Grand Design Shop competition of 2016, offers a wide range of publications on fine art, design, architecture, photography and poetry, with the aim of promoting the work of young artists and cultural opinion leaders. It is regularly used as an exhibition venue, e.g. during the cartoon festival Lustr.

185 ARTMAP

Vojtěšská 18
New Town ②
+420 773 679 612
artmap.cz

Originally started out as a project to map contemporary art events in Prague galleries by two arty called brothers Tomáš and Petr Hrůza. Gradually ARTMAP evolved into a bookstore selling a wide range of books on design, architecture and graphic art, which also happens to have a colourful children's section. Do not forget to pick up your own copy of the map.

184 PAGEFIVE

The 5 best places to find UNUSUAL SOUVENIRS

186 **PRAGTIQUE**
AT: PASÁŽ PLATÝZ
Národní 37
Old Town ①
pragtique.com

Enough with the Matryoshkas and kitsch fridge magnets. Here you can find creative handcrafted souvenirs designed by leading Czech contemporary artists including a blueprint Prague panorama mug, tote bags depicting the Castle in traditional mosaic style, postcards of the popular Náplavka embankment and much more.

187 **SKOBA**
Křížkovského 10 (entry from Ševčíkova 4)
Žižkov ⑤
+420 775 314 592
iskoba.cz

Feel the need to write down all your great memories of Prague? Then pay a visit to Václav Pišoft, a graphic designer who made a career switch to (note)book binding, using only recycled paper and textiles. Your old favourite shirt or tablecloth can become a personalised stationery item.

188 **ANALOGUE**
Vlašská 10
Lesser Town ③
+420 603 530 035
analogue.cz

This quirky gallery is bound to cheer up fans of analogue photography and lomography in particular. Classic or contemporary pieces, simple pinhole cameras, filters, lighting and accessories, you name it, they have it. You can even rent a dark room here to develop your Prague snapshots.

189 KOH-I-NOOR

Na Poříčí 23
New Town ①
+420 739 329 697
koh-i-noor.cz

On the ground floor of Bílá Labuť department store you will find an official stationery shop selling all possible KOH-I-NOOR products. Since 1790, the company has developed a range of products for artists, schools and offices, including drawing pencils, leads, sepia blocks, inks, charcoals, oils and watercolour. Their 1500 graphite pencil is the most popular pencil in the world.

190 THUN

Vinohradská 61
Vinohrady ④
+420 222 230 579
thun.cz

A great place for top class Czech porcelain and glass at fair prices: from traditional cibulák blueprints and elegant Bernadotte dinnerware to minimalistic Scandinavian style tea sets. A carafe made of glass containing 24% of lead oxide creates thousands of rainbow prisms and would be a unique piece to take home. Check your luggage weight allowance first though.

190 THUN

The 5 most interesting
MARKETS

191 **HOLEŠOVICE MARKET**
Bubenské nábřeží 13
Holešovice ⑧
+420 220 800 592
prazska-trznice.cz

Check out Hall 22, with a great selection of fruit and vegetables. It has a small stand selling Uzbek specialities, next to the entrance you'll find a Slovak bakery with cow and sheep dairy products. Hall 28 is where you'll find the Moravian Wine Bank, which has 800 different bottles on offer.

192 **SAPA**
Libušská 126
Libuš
+420 604 565 920
www.sapamapa.cz

'Kính chào qúy khách' reads the inscription on the gate of SAPA market, which the locals nicknamed Little Hanoi. Its massive grounds are not only for shopping though. This is also the cultural centre of the city's large Vietnamese community. They even elect their own Miss! Look for Hue Xra to sample the best *Bún bò Hue*.

193 **FARMERS' MARKETS**
(various locations)
farmarsketrziste.cz
farmarske-trhy.cz

After two decades of shopping in supermarkets, the Czechs have gone back to basics – buying from local farmers. There are three main market locations: Jiřího z Poděbrad hosts the market on Wednesdays, Thursdays and Fridays, on Saturday head to Náplavka or Vítězné náměstí in Dejvice.

194 KOLBENKA BLĚSÍ TRHY

U Elektry
Vysočany
+420 733 785 540
blesitrhy.cz

Prague's largest flea market is held every weekend (from 6 am till 3 pm) in an industrial district next to a railway. In this 50.000-sq m market you can find anything from tools to musical instruments, as well as crockery and bikes, animal horns and Christmas decorations. All you need is some patience as you rummage through everything.

195 MINT MARKET

Bubenské nábřeží 13
Holešovice ⑧
+420 728 230 430
mintmarket.cz

A project inspired by London's Camden Town and Bangkok's weekend markets. The market is open every Saturday (except during the summer break) in Hall 13 of the town market grounds. Expect local food and delicatessen, independent fashion labels, design, organic cosmetics, books, music and various workshops.

191 HOLEŠOVICE MARKET

5 *tempting*
DELI SHOPS

196 **OLYMPIA**
Radhošťská 1
Vinohrady ⑤
+420 724 325 502
recky-obchod.cz

The place to shop for various Greek products, such as olives (oil), yoghurt, seafood, halloumi cheese, honey, wine and Retsina wine. Their motto 'Taste Greece' is matched by the food on offer and the friendliness of the staff.

197 **SVÁČEK**
Štefánikova 33
Smíchov ⑦
+420 606 389 765
lahudkarstvisvacek.cz

One of the biggest delis in town (it has two other branches), offering a fine selection of cured hams and meats (from Italy, France, Spain or the Balkans), cheese and antipasti. They also sell traditional Czech products, including wines. Very helpful sales assistants.

198 **TESORI D'ABRUZZO**
Klimentská 34 (passage)
New Town ②
+420 608 367 403

Nowhere else in Prague will you find such a large concentration of truffle specialities per square metre. In this tiny store Chiara Gregoraci sells organic products from her native Abruzzo region, ranging from pasta to cheeses and aperitif goodies, which all contain 'the black diamond'. She will gladly recommend a wine to pair with your purchase.

199 ZLATÝ KŘÍŽ

Jungmannova 34
New Town ①
+420 222 519 451
lahudkyzlatykriz.cz

This place looks rather outdated, with its tired-looking sales assistants and faded photos on the walls. The oldest delicatessen in Prague offers more than 50 types of *chlebíček* and is packed every day. Their mayonnaise celeriac salad is legendary, but they charge by weight so feel free to try others, too. Eat-in or take-away.

200 MERCATO

Pobřežní 42
Karlín ⑥
+420 731 636 318
mercato.cz

This deli bistro opened to promote the culinary products used in two upmarket restaurants that are part of the same group. Here you can enjoy wine, cheeses, sausages and oils that are sourced from small and medium-sized European producers at take-away prices. Try the smoked paprika, which makes an amazing addition to all Spanish recipes.

The 5 best places to LIQUOR-UP

201 **WAREHOUSE #1**
Sokolovská 105
Karlín ⑥
+420 608 520 526
warehouse1.cz

This retail store is located just under the headquarters of a company specialising in the import of quality spirits. Need a bottle to spice up a party, a triple A wine or something for your private collection (a rare bottle of 40-year-old Japanese whisky)? They have it all and even more.

202 **TRETTER'S GALLERY SPIRITS SHOP**
Kozí 9
Old Town ①
+420 224 815 848
tretters-spirits.cz

A place to buy fancy bartender equipment, as well as premium, investment and auction alcohol, exclusive wines and champagnes. They introduced a 'shared bottle concept' – after paying your share online you can have a taste without having to pay for an entire bottle – in order to avoid applying for a bar licence.

203 **MEAD MUSEUM**
Na Zderaze 14
New Town ②
+420 775 633 077
muzeummedoviny.cz

Mead supposedly is the oldest liquor in the world. This small museum and store has more than a hundred different types, a third of which are sourced from Slovak producers. Up to twenty varieties can be tasted every day, including special cocktails, such as Mead Mojito.

204 ABSINTHERIE

Jilská 7
Old Town ①
+420 224 251 999
absintherie.cz

Sip, don't quaff this highly alcoholic spirit, which is also sometimes named the green fairy. Learn more about its history, the difference between Swiss and Czech absinth and try a seasonal absinth ice cream. And don't worry, the psychedelic images on the walls are really there. Or *are* they?

205 BECHEROVKA

Václav Havel Airport
becherovka.com

Becherovka is a traditional liquor, a secret mix of twenty herbs and spices. If you did not have the opportunity to taste this special digestive, then do try it before you leave. It is great, both pure and chilled or in cocktails, the list of which can be found on their website.

The 5 most

PECULIAR SHOPS

206 **U SALVÁTORA**
Náprstkova 2
Old Town ①
+420 222 221 161
prodejnausalvatora.cz

This family spice shop has been around for almost 50 years. With its sweet scent, wooden panelling and an antique till, the atmosphere is reminiscent of the good old days. They are renowned for their special meat mixes, but you can also buy different kinds of salts, from Himalayan pink to Cornish, here too.

207 **GUMA**
Ječná 24
New Town ②
+420 224 918 411
gumapraha.cz

This shop has sold an unusually wide range of rubber goods, foams, adhesives, sealants, plastics and linoleum since 1937. Do you need a water tap seal, a piece of hose or a raincoat? They have it all, as well as a fantastic collection of famous inflatable toys by Libuše Niklová.

208 **MILITARY ANTIQUES**
Charvátova 11
New Town ①
+420 602 294 134

This funky store just off Národní looks like something between an old arsenal and a museum. They sell everything from leather Gestapo coats, gas masks, flasks, cartridges, helmets and sabres. Including the type that defeated Napoleon at Waterloo.

209 ÚJEZD ROPE SHOP

Vítězná 10
Lesser Town ③
+420 776 886 449
www.provaznictvi.cz

Some two hundred years ago the current owner's great-great-grandfather started a small store by the Vltava River – a natural place where you'd expect to buy ropes and nets. After the Smíchov lock was built, before WWI, his business flourished. You will never realise in how many areas of life you need rope until you visit.

210 AZBUKA CHUTÍ

Štefánikova 25
Smíchov ⑦
+420 777 340 445

Azbuka (Eastern alphabet) of taste. You may think that this store has a rather limited offering. And yet many Russian speaking customers love its good variety of caviar and pickled fish. Wash it down with sparkling wine from Crimea, red wines from Georgia or Armenian cognac.

207 GUMA

5 *tantalising*
SWEETSHOPS

211 **SAINT TROPEZ**
Vodičkova 30
New Town ②
+420 603 333 338
cukrarnatropez.cz

Finding this place in the maze of covered passages can be difficult but the reward is worth it. With a family tradition in hand-crafted sweets, this little gem has a branch on the French Côte d'Azur, so its influence is obvious. They organise small workshops to share their *savoir-faire*.

212 **ELVÍRA**
Zelená 4
Dejvice ⑨
+420 776 596 481

Ordering a cake here results in several dilemmas – cheesecake, *Eszterhazy* cake or plain chocolate? And then – should you just admire its stunning beauty or actually eat it? The friendly youthful staff will help you out.

213 **PERNÍČKŮV SEN**
Haštalská 21
Old Town ①
+420 607 773 350
pernickuvsen.cz

Hansel and Gretel would have loved this store full of fragrant gingerbread. No witches lurking here though, just two friendly sisters-in-law and the amazing fragrance of cinnamon and aniseed. Try their *sakrajda*, a strudel with plum jam and walnuts, with your coffee.

214 CHOCO-CAFÉ

Klimentská 34
New Town ①
+420 212 242 519
choco-cafe.cz

A place for real chocolate connoisseurs, with chocolates listed by origin. From the Americas or Madagascar, with ginger, fruit, alcohol, sugar-free or in the form of pralines. If you overdose on the spot, then stock up on their homemade chocolate bars for later.

215 IF CAFÉ

Belgická 30
Vinohrady ④
+420 608 773 399
ifcafe.cz

Iveta Fabešová fell in love with everything French a long time ago. She prepares delicate pastries in her cafe, including the increasingly popular macarons. The sweet smell will hit you as you walk in, guiding your nose to the kitchen where all the magic happens. Ask about their antidepressant paste made of pistachios or salty caramel.

211 SAINT TROPEZ

5 delicious ICE-CREAM places

216 PURO GELATO

Na Hrobci 1
New Town ②
+420 721 438 209
purogelato.cz

If you decide to stroll along Náplavka, then arm yourself with a cone of something tasty. At Gelato Puro they prepare a variety of gelato and sorbet flavours daily in small batches from fresh natural ingredients. They take their work very seriously, so make sure you do not call it ice cream.

217 CRÈME DE LA CRÈME

Husova 12
Old Town ①
+420 224 211 035
cremecreme.cz

Only you can judge whether they really serve the best ice cream in Prague as they claim. Try lavender or strawberry-basil on a hot day or vegan pancakes in winter. A welcome tasty break on your way from the Old Town Square and the Charles Bridge.

218 PARLOR

Křižíkova 37
Karlín ⑥
+420 724 518 080
parlor.cz

On his travels through the USA Lukáš Prokop came across the ice-cream sandwich concept, fell in love and decided to bring it home. At Parlor they bake their own cookies and use the best ice cream in town. Their 'knock-off' gin selection is equally popular with the neighbourhood's office workers.

219 **ZMRZLINÁŘ**
Slezská 15
Vinohrady ④
+420 733 785 657
zmrzlinar.cz

After his favourite Italian gelateria closed down, Darek Hrivňák decided his home town could no longer be deprived of this delicacy. His gelato proved a hit and led him to open a shop in Prague. Choosing just one of the many flavours might be tricky, but feel free to ask if you can taste before ordering. Try something different too. Ever tasted sea buckthorn sorbet?

220 **AMATO**
Heřmanova 61
Holešovice ⑧
+420 223 016 223
gelateriaamato.cz

After 15 years of working for a multinational corporation, Palermo-born Pietro Amato decided to follow his passion for sweets. His mix of milk and seasonal fruit from local farmers with Sicilian nuts and citruses soon was a hit with the locals. Salty caramel is still the bestselling flavour but he experiments weekly, creating new, surprising flavours, such as gorgonzola or beetroot.

219 ZMRZLINÁŘ

The 5 best

BUTCHER SHOPS

221 **PRESTO MEAT MARKET**
Vítkova 11
Karlín ⑥
+420 732 326 666
meat-market.cz

An increasingly popular concept consisting of a butcher's shop next to a gourmet bistro. Here they sell aged beef, lamb and quality chicken from Czech farms. If you are unsure how to properly prepare your lovely meat, then join one of their cooking/barbecue lessons.

222 **PRAŽSKÉ ŘEZNICTVÍ**
Vinohradská 108
Vinohrady ⑤
+420 725 157 980
prazskereznictvi.cz

A butcher who is also a champion of traditional Czech cooking. They sell a selection of high-quality products, and also recommend grandma's best recipes. You can find rabbit, cockerel, chicken livers or beef for your steak tartare here, as well as sausages and cheese. The bistro corner serves tasty fast food.

223 **U DOLEJŠÍCH**
Na náměstí 97
Davle
+420 257 770 039
dolejsi.cz

If you do not mind travelling out of town for top class meat, then head to Davle. Since 1901, the Dolejších butcher family have been running a reputable company known for its quality and openness to customers. Their hams and sausages are simply divine.

224 **THE REAL MEAT SOCIETY**
Náplavní 5
New Town ②
+420 739 022 597
trms.cz

'From nose to tail' is the rule here, meaning that no part of an animal should be wasted. The organic butcher's shop of Michaela and Paul Day only works with small farms whose animals live outside and walk from their field to the slaughterhouse, without having to undergo the stress of travel.

225 **NAŠE MASO**
Dlouhá 39
Old Town ①
+420 222 311 378
nasemaso.ambi.cz

The top class meat used in the Ambiente restaurant group is sold here as well as the aged beef of Czech spotted cattle, the juicy pork of Přestice pigs and homemade sausages. For takeaway meat purchases enter the passage and find the store on the left. The long queue out front is for the bistro, whose delicious food you can smell out in the street.

225 NAŠE MASO

SAINT JAMES BASILICA

30 BUILDINGS TO ADMIRE

5 *unique* CHURCHES

226 **MOST SACRED HEART OF OUR LORD**
Nám. Jiřího z Poděbrad
Vinohrady ④
+420 222 727 713
srdcepane.cz

Built by the very religious Slovenian architect Josip Plečnik, this church combines various different trends in architecture. Its interior features simple geometric shapes. The massive wooden ceiling is suspended from a complex metal structure that is hidden in the attic. The plastic façade plays with shadows and changes depending on the sun's position.

227 **SAINT JAMES BASILICA**
Malá Štupartská 6
Old Town ①
+420 224 828 814
praha.minorite.cz

The inconspicuous outside appearance of this large basilica sharply contrasts with its gilded decor. It also features a famous organ that dates from 1705. You can hear its 4 manuals, 91 speaking tops and 8277 pipes every Sunday from 10 am.

228 **EVANGELICAL CHURCH**
Náměstí Před Bateriemi
Střešovice ③

This nameless church is an important Functionalist monument built in 1930. The architect's intention was to create a place of worship reminiscent of Christian basilicas. The purity of style makes this a dominating feature in the surrounding residential area, with its large villas.

229 JUBILEE SYNAGOGUE

Jeruzalémská 7
New Town ①
+420 224 800 849
synagogue.cz

The most recent synagogue, built as a compensation for three synagogues that were demolished when the slums in Josefov were cleared at the end of the 19th century. This very generously proportioned building with its stunning Moorish style interior can be visited from April to October after paying a small entrance fee.

230 SAINT GABRIEL CHURCH

Holečkova 10
Smíchov ⑦
+420 244 463 675
beuron.cz

On the southern slope of Petřín Hill stands Saint Gabriel Monastery and its neo-Romanesque basilica. It belonged to the Benedictine order, which decorated its interior before fleeing in 1919. The exquisite Beuronese murals can only be seen during Mass (every Sunday at 11.15 am) or during a guided tour arranged beforehand.

227 SAINT JAMES BASILICA

5 *magnificent* ART NOUVEAU BUILDINGS

231 **HOTEL CENTRAL**
Hybernská 10
New Town ①
+420 225 022 000
kkhotels.com/en/prague/hotel-central

This impressive hotel was the very first Art Nouveau building in Prague. It features lovely floral patterns on the façade, an ornate staircase and elevator area. Formerly a theatre, its main hall unfortunately was subdivided into two floors to accommodate a meeting room and a restaurant. Walk in for a good look.

232 **ČECHŮV BRIDGE**
Connects Letná Park and the Jewish Quarter
Old Town ①

Maybe the shortest of Prague's bridges, but also the largest ornate construction in the country. Note the four genii statues that are perched on the glazed iron lanterns atop 18-metre pylons. Six-headed bronze water monsters and women carrying torches are suspended over the water.

233 **MAIN TRAIN STATION**
Wilsonova 8
New Town ①

The station's recently renovated main hall is home to the Fanta Café (a tribute to its architect). Under the dome passengers are reminded in golden letters of their arrival to 'the Mother of Cities'. Numerous heraldry refers to Czech towns connected to Prague by rail in the old days.

234 SAINT VOJTĚCH CHURCH

U Meteoru
Libeň
+420 283 892 404

Remarkable for its system of vertical masonry structures combined with intricately shaped wooden roof trusses. Open to the public during mass, on Tuesdays and Saturdays at 5 pm, Sundays at 10 am. Across the road stands another Art Nouveau structure worth checking out, called Sokol House.

235 BÍLEK'S VILLA

Mickiewiczova 1
Hradčany ③
+420 233 323 631
ghmp.cz

Astonishment is the name of František Bílek's gigantic statue in his workshop, but also your feeling once you enter his villa built in the mystic Art Nouveau style. The family's living quarters had no doors to allow energy flows, while the building's temple-like appearance stems from Bílek's confession, avowing Christian reformism.

233 MAIN TRAIN STATION

The 5 most exquisite
VILLAS

236 **VILLA ROTHMAYER**
U Pátě baterie 50
Břevnov ③
+420 224 312 012
muzeumprahy.cz

The design of architect Otto Rothmayer's family home was directly inspired by his teacher Plečnik, for whom he carried out major transformations at Prague castle. Materials 'borrowed' from there can be found all over his villa, which has a rather Mediterranean atmosphere. Can be visited in small groups after reservation.

237 **VILLA PELLÉ**
Pelléova 10
Bubeneč ⑨
+420 224 326 180
villapelle.cz

In spite of its neo-Renaissance style, this villa is named after a French general, not after the Italian football player. Its façade is lavishly decorated with sgraffito technique and well-preserved remainders of stucco. The four floors are shared between an art gallery and a cultural centre

238 **TRMAL VILLA**
Vilová 11
Strašnice
+420 274 777 308
trmalovavila.cz

For this villa, the famous architect Jan Kotěra drew inspiration from English country manors. The result is a unique example of Art Nouveau geometric ornaments combined with rural architecture and Slavic traditions. The colourful wooden panelling of the central staircase is simply spectacular.

239 VILLA MÜLLER

Nad Hradním vodojemem 14
Střešovice ③
+420 224 312 012
muzeumprahy.cz

Using Swiss marble and Parisian fabrics, Adolf Loos clearly designed this villa to impress and represent. It is austere, yet luxurious and practical, its outside functionalist appearance contrasts with a generous internal layout. A joint ticket for the Rothmayer villa entitles you to a discount.

240 VILLA AMERICA/DVOŘÁK MUSEUM

Ke Karlovu 20
New Town ②
+420 224 918 013
nm.cz

When it was built by Kilian Ignaz Dientzenhofer, the main architect of the local Baroque era, this summerhouse was still located far outside the city. Its main hall resembles a temple to the muses, with frescoes depicting Greek gods. It frequently hosts concerts, as the Museum of Music has installed the permanent exhibition on Antonín Dvořák here.

239 VILLA MÜLLER

5 *hidden*
COVERED PASSAGES

241 LUCERNA, ROKOKO AND U NOVÁKŮ
Vodičkova 36
New Town ②

These three passages that are just a few steps off busy Vodičkova Street have turned the entire block into Emmental. Bump into parents escorting their offspring to a cinema matinée, teenagers about to attend their prom or rockers heading to a live concert. Look for Saint Wenceslas sitting on a dead horse.

242 SVĚTOZOR AND U STÝBLŮ
Vodičkova 39
New Town ②

These two interconnected passages could not be more contrasting – while Světozor swarms with cinema-goers, ice-cream and sushi-eaters, U Stýblů has hardly any cultural life left. Take a break there and look up to appreciate the 1947 Tesla mosaic advert (!) and the light that falls in through the glass brick ceiling.

243 KORUNA PALACE
Václavské náměstí 1
New Town ①

This late Art Nouveau palace was built for a bank and included a spa, a cinema and a cabaret. Between the wars people would happily queue here to get *chlebíčeks* and lemonade from the first vending machine. Today it could tell sad stories about how far privatisation can go.

244 **CZECH DESIGN PASSAGE**
Na Příkopě 24
New Town ①

This passage under the Czech National Bank showcases the work of emerging, progressive talent every three months. Window-shop for furniture, jewellery or tableware, attend one of the workshops or meet authors. But people-watching from the trendy cafe and feasting on a cake is also an option of course.

245 **ADRIA PALACE**
Národní 38
New Town ①

This marvel of Rondocubism was built in the 1920s by an Italian insurance company called Riunione Adriatica di Securità. In the middle of its façade stands a giant statue called *Seafaring*, the interior is decorated with marble and copper. Find the inner B staircase and take a ride in the ancient elevator.

242 **SVĚTOZOR AND U STÝBLŮ**

The 5 most interesting REMNANTS OF COMMUNISM

246 **HOTEL INTERNACIONAL**
Koulova 15
Dejvice ⑨
+420 296 537 111
internationalprague.cz

The largest representative of the Socialist realism style in Prague. Its basement concealed a nuclear shelter, which could accommodate 600 people for two weeks. This was later turned into staff cloakrooms. The red five-pointed star – the symbol of Soviet communism – was preserved on the steeple, but was painted green.

247 **KOTVA DEPARTMENT STORE**
Náměstí republiky 8
Old Town ①
+420 224 801 111
od-kotva.cz

Fans of Brutalist architecture will love the floor plan of black raw concrete blocks, set into multiple intertwined hexagons to symbolise the prosperity and abundance of socialism. Amazing views of the Old Town from the rooftop terrace bar.

248 **STRAHOV STADIUM**
Vaníčkova 6
Břevnov ③

The largest stadium in the world for an audience of 250.000. Its vast inner surface area of nine football pitches was used for so called 'spartakiads', mass gymnastics events to celebrate the Red Army's liberation of Czechoslovakia. Maintenance proofed too costly lately, making it a favourite urbex location.

249 FEDERAL ASSEMBLY BUILDING

Vinohradská 1
Vinohrady ④②

The former headquarters of the Federal Assembly. In the 1990s, it was the home of Radio Free Europe and now it has become a part of the National Museum. Built in the late 1960s, curiously enough it used the same extension Vierendeel truss technology that was used around the same time for the FBI headquarters building in Washington.

250 NEW STAGE OF THE NATIONAL THEATRE

Národní 4
New Town ②
+420 224 901 448
narodni-divadlo.cz

The New Stage of the National Theatre focuses on contemporary projects. It was built in the 1980s using more than four thousand glass bricks to obtain better acoustics. On your way up to the Nona Café (on the first floor), don't forget to admire the impressive sculpture that extends up through the staircase along the entire height of the building.

250 NEW STAGE OF THE NATIONAL THEATRE

5 hidden gems of
CUBISM

251 **KOVAŘOVIC VILLA**
Libušina 3
Vyšehrad ②

Inspired by the works of Braque and Picasso, its façade creates interesting shadows and animations. The villa itself, and the garden layout, the flower beds, the surrounding fence and even the steps are Cubist designs. The best view is from the front, on the corner of Vnislavova Street and Rašínovo nábřeží.

252 **U NEKLANA**
Přemyslova 11
Vyšehrad ②

This humble corner apartment building resembles a ship anchored under the Vyšehrad ramparts. The original plans were much more ornate, but the conservative pre-war city council would not hear of it. The most striking elements are the hexagonal windows, through which you can peep inside.

253 **CUBIST LAMP POST**
Jungmannovo náměstí
New Town ①

Between numbers 13 and 14 stands the only cubist lamp post in the world. The original geometrical concrete pile of truncated cones, half-lamp half-bench, is now kept in the Prague City Gallery. An authentic copy now stands near the church entrance.

254 **HOUSE OF THE BLACK MADONNA**

Ovocný trh 19
Old Town ①
+420 778 543 901
czkubismus.cz

What happens if you turn a cubist painting into real 3D? That was the question Josef Gočár asked himself when he decided to apply this artistic principle in architecture and interior design. Visit the Czech Cubism exhibition and stop in the Grand Orient Café to feast on a cubist cream puff dessert.

255 **ŽIŽKOV BETLEHEM CHAPEL**

Prokopova 4
Žižkov ⑤

The golden banner above the altar claims that 'Truth Shall Prevail!'. For a Protestant chapel its interior is rather ornate, with walls covered with geometric patterns in warm tones. It is also surprising to find such a gem nestled in the greenery of an ordinary courtyard. Stop in on Monday evenings to attend choir rehearsals.

254 HOUSE OF THE BLACK MADONNA

NATIONAL LIBRARY OF TECHNOLOGY

FREE DOM
SOCIETY
POLITICS
BIBLE
GOOGLE
REFORM
TRAGEDY
STATISTICS
3
4

75 PLACES TO DISCOVER PRAGUE

5 *breath-taking* VIEWS

256 **HANAVSKY PAVILION**
Letenské sady 173
Holešovice ⑧

This impressive iron structure was built to represent Slovak ironworks during the Jubilee Exhibition of 1891. Today it houses a tourist trap restaurant but from its terrace you enjoy a magnificent panoramic view of the nine bridges that span across the Vltava River.

257 **SAINT NICHOLAS BELL TOWER**
Malostranské náměstí
Lesser Town ③

The most impressive example of Prague Baroque and Baroque in general north of the Alps, which also coincidentally was the last town crier's tower to be built in Prague. Funnily enough, it belonged to the city, rather than the Church. To enjoy a spectacular 360° view of the entire city centre climb up its 299 steps.

258 **DÍVČÍ HRADY**
GPS: 50.0511897N, 14.4042803E
Tetínská
Radlice ⑦
(bus stop Dívčí hrady)

A place filled with mystery, where the fortress of the Maidens once stood on the riverbank opposite Vyšehrad before the uprising of the Czech Estates. It was subsequently replaced by a water tower, but the views are just as beautiful. A perfect spot for a romantic picnic.

259 **PRAGUE TUNNELS COMMAND CENTRE**
Šermířská 11
Břevnov ③
(Station Strahov bus stop)

This cube-like building's balcony offers a panoramic view to the south and east. You can see Pakrác, a modern neighbourhood with its apartment buildings and a city prison. To its right you will spot the basilica of Saint Peter and Paul inside Vyšehrad Fortress, the former seat of the Kings of Bohemia.

260 **STRAHOV MONASTERY**
Strahovské nádvoří
Strahov ③
(Pohořelec tram stop)

As you enter the courtyard of Strahov Monastery keep to the right and continue to walk towards Peklo Restaurant, then take the first left along the vineyard. This little path will lead you to what is arguably the most spectacular view in Prague, with the Castle, Lesser Town, Old Town and Žižkov. Don't forget to breathe.

260 STRAHOV MONASTERY

5 *places to* UNDERSTAND CZECH HISTORY

261 LIBUŠE AND PŘEMYSL

Přemyslova 5-7
Vyšehrad ②

The portals of these two doorways feature the shortened legend of Princess Libuše and her ploughman husband Přemysl. She found him through a prophecy and had him brought to her directly from the field. Together they founded the House of Přemyslid, the first Czech royal dynasty, and lived happily ever after in Vyšehrad Castle.

262 NEW TOWN HALL

Karlovo náměstí 1
New Town ②
+420 224 948 229

The movement for the reformation of the Catholic Church started as early as the 15th century. Jan Hus and his followers had a rather unconventional way of dealing with anyone who opposed their ideas. They were responsible for the Prague Defenestration – during which the entire city council including the major were cast out of the town-hall window. The courtyard has a trendy cafe.

263 WHITE MOUNTAIN

GPS: 50.0783294N, 14.3192047E
Karlovarská 1677
Břevnov
(Bílá Hora tram stop)

Right next to the tram terminus stands the Church of Our Lady Victorious, which replaced a small chapel where the remains of soldiers which were found in the nearby battle field were buried. A few hundred metres up the road, a little mound features a monument that witnessed one of the most crushing defeats in Czech history.

264 THE CHURCH OF THE PARATROOPERS

Resslova 9a
New Town ②
+420 224 920 686
pamatnik-heydrichiady.cz

Bullet holes in the crypt's outer wall are a reminder of what followed after the assassination of Reinhard Heydrich in 1942. The Czechs paid dearly for this act of resistance, which was orchestrated by the government in exile. However, it clearly showed the Allies on which side of the barricades they were standing.

265 STALIN

Letenské sady
Letná ⑧
(Čechův most tram stop)

In November 1962, Prague's citizens heard glasses in their cupboards rattle. Yet it was no earthquake, as many thought, but an explosion secretly disposing of the 17.000-ton Stalin monument. It only stood there shortly, but until today this place is a reminder of the dangers of an ideological personality cult.

The 5 most fascinating INDUSTRIAL HERITAGE SITES

266 **NÁKLADOVÉ NÁDRAŽÍ ŽIŽKOV**

Jana Želivského 2
Žižkov ⑤
nakladovenadrazi zizkov.com

This historic rail freight station almost made way for luxury apartments before being listed as a cultural monument in 2010. Now home to the National Film Archives it hosts cultural events including outdoor cinema, concerts and exhibitions. Take a seat on the tracks, with a drink, and admire industrial heritage in its purest form.

267 **OLD WATER TREATMENT PLANT**

Papírenská 6
Bubeneč ⑨
+420 777 790 219
stara-cistirna.cz

The 100-year-old sewage treatment plant which was designed by a British civil engineer opened its doors to public only recently. Explore old machinery, stroll through the remediated sewage mains and if you feel more adventurous go rafting or climb up the ventilation smokestack with ropes. Warm clothes, cash only.

268 NEGRELLI VIADUCT

Prvního pluku
Karlín ⑥
viaduktkreativni.cz

Prague's second oldest railway bridge. With its 87 arches, it was the longest in Europe for 60 years following its construction. After decades of neglect, the city allowed to revive it to provide shelter for dancefloors, playgrounds, cafes and galleries, rather than smelly carparks and dog toilets.

269 HOLEŠOVICE BREWERY

Komunardů 42
Holešovice ⑧

A high brick chimney contrasts sharply with the snow-white façades of the surrounding buildings. In 1897, the First Prague Burgers' Brewery was founded here. Nowadays you will find offices, apartments and shops set around a small central courtyard with various rusty piano statues.

270 MARINA

V Přístavu
Holešovice ⑧

This dead tributary of the Vltava River recently attracted a lot of attention from real estate developers. Large apartment blocks have been built here, overlooking a plethora of rusty cargo ships that are moored in the old industrial port. For a more authentic experience explore the other side where the ship repair docks are located.

The 5 best sightseeing trips by
PUBLIC TRANSPORT

271 **BUS 194**
dpp.cz

This line is served by a minibus, since it needs to wind its way through the narrow streets of the city centre. The shuttle makes the journey between Petrské and Haštalské Squares twice every hour, then continues to Pařížská shopping street, Mariánské Square connecting with the city hall and National Library and then over the bridge to Malostranská.

272 **TRAM 23**
dpp.cz

This nostalgic line is served by the popular Prague-made Tatra T3 tramcars, with over 14.000 trams sold worldwide. It connects several attractions in the centre including the New Town Hall, the National Theatre, Lesser Town or the Castle. Tram 23 departs every 15 to 30 minutes.

273 **TRAM 41**
dpp.cz

Has a similar itinerary as line 23, but only runs from March till November on weekends. With a special ticket, costing 35 CZK, you can ride a historical tram from the period between the world wars. It runs once hourly, from noon till 5 pm.

274 FUNICULAR

dpp.cz

Want to take a closer look at the little Eiffel Tower on top of Petřín hill? The funicular will take you there every day from 9 am till 11.30 pm. The 24 CZK ticket is worth every penny as it saves you the 130-metre uphill trek. Get off at Nebozízek for a romantic garden restaurant with a great view.

275 FERRIES

prazskebenatky.cz

In Prague's city centre, there is a bridge almost every few hundred metres. In addition, several small ferries connect both river banks. They usually run from April till October and work with regular transport tickets.

274 FUNICULAR

5 *charming*
HIDDEN COURTYARDS

276 **HOLLAR**
Smetanovo nábřeží 6
Old Town ①

This courtyard belongs to the faculty of Social Sciences. You will need to ask the person at reception to let you in, explaining that you are visiting the cafe. After checking out this pleasant student eatery in a former garage, feel free to roam around the building and courtyard with its many balconies.

277 **HOUSE AT THE GOLDEN RING**
Týnská 6
Old Town ①

Walk past the reception of Prague's City Museum into a small courtyard between two medieval buildings. During the summer it transforms into the terrace of a literary cafe, so while you sip your beverage you can admire its Tuscan pillars and Gothic vaults.

278 **FLORENTINUM**
Na Florenci 15
New Town ①

In the middle of this shopping passage, you will find the entrance to a courtyard. The first one is full of glass and concrete, but if you walk through, another space will open up in front of you, behind Desfour Palace. Its garden was transformed into a peaceful oasis.

279 **POST OFFICE HEADQUARTERS**

Jindřišská 14
New Town ①
+420 221 131 445

Prague's central post office opened here in 1874. Since then, the courtyard has been skilfully transformed into a main hall. On the first floor you can visit an exhibition on the history of postal services. The building is connected to the world's last municipal pneumatic post system in operation, which is 55 kilometres long.

280 **U HALÁNKŮ**

Betlémské náměstí 1
Old Town ①

This is the courtyard of a former brewery and distillery. The buildings were acquired in 1826 by the Fingerhut family. Their son Vojta Náprstek, a philanthropist and patriot who had his name changed to the Czech translation, established the Museum of Asian, African and American cultures.

276 **HOLLAR**

5 *unexpected* SHORTCUTS

281 **UP VLAŠSKÁ STREET TO PETŘÍN HILL**
Lesser Town ③

To make the most of your viewing experience in Big Strahov Garden, take the stairs up from Vlašská Street, that start around the corner off Lobkovický Palace (the German embassy). Avoid turning around until you are on the top of the hill to be utterly astonished at the view.

282 **NA LIBUŠINCE**
Vyšehrad ②

Another workout, that will be rewarded with some spectacular vistas. Walk up the stairs toward the Vyšehrad fortress ramparts, pausing briefly on the balcony halfway to look around. Catch your breath and give your legs a rest when you arrive at the top. There is a bar right in front of Saint Peter and Paul Basilica.

283 **ŽIŽKOV TO KARLÍN TUNNEL**
⑤⑥

This pedestrian tunnel connects Thámova Street in Karlín with Tachovské Square in Žižkov. Try to briefly stop in the middle, where neither end of the tunnel can be seen, to test its acoustics. Funnily enough, the tunnel is located along the Camino di Santiago pilgrimage route.

284 NUSELSKÉ SCHODY

Šafaříkova 1
Vinohrady ④

A series of stairs (182 in total) descending from Vinohrady to Nusle. At the top of the staircase you will see some spectacular villas. At the bottom stands a unique timber house that was built in the 1930s for a rich mine owner. During WWII, it was used as accommodation for the Hitlerjugend and nowadays it sadly is rundown.

285 KAMZÍKOVÁ

Old Town ①

As a quick escape from the Old Town Square, turn onto Celetná and find the entrance between numbers 8 and 10. It will take you into Kamzíková, where you will find the 'House at the Black Peacock'. There used to be a famous brothel here, which was frequented by Otto van Bismarck and Gustav Mahler (among others).

281 UP VLAŠSKÁ STREET TO PETŘÍN HILL

5

QUAINT LITTLE STREETS

286 **NOVÝ SVĚT**
Hradčany ③

Its name, meaning 'New World', refers to the contrast with the pompous architecture of the neighbouring Castle. The street's tiny houses were the homes of the poorest families and artists. Go before 7 pm and pop into a family cafe in number 2 after taking a sneak peek into the public garden opposite number 11.

287 **SLAVÍČKOVA**
Bubeneč ⑨

These graceful lime trees dwarf some valuable architectural gems. Most of these villas were built for the country's intellectual elite at the turn of the 19th and 20th centuries. Some aspired to look like English manor houses, while others embraced Art Nouveau, but all deserve your time and attention.

288 **NA KOCOURKÁCH**
Střešovice ③

This street is all that remains of a former workers' colony, with houses dug partially into a mass of sandstone. Some say its name refers to the cobble stones ('cat heads' in Czech), but in fact it is named after the vineyard that used to be here.

289 U OBECNÍHO DVORA

Old Town ①

Its name implies the existence of a municipal yard, with city stables, barns and carriage parks. The spacious grounds were used for the first fire brigade trainings and later for the fire station. The Romantic painter Josef Mánes, who was born here in 1820, would hardly recognise it today, after the large scale clearance of these slums just before WWI.

290 ZLATÁ

Old Town ①

At Anenské náměstí step under a small gate with a statue on top of it into the Golden Lane. It curves around the former Saint Anne's convent whose church was turned into a cultural centre by Václav Havel. As you reach Liliová you can spot the second lap of Zlatá about 5 metres to your right.

286 NOVÝ SVĚT

The 5 most

PICTURESQUE SQUARES

291 **SAINT PETER'S CHURCH**
Petrská
New Town ①

This little open space around the former Romanesque Basilica of Saint Peter, its garden and bell tower recently became a very hip area. Cosy restaurants now have terraces in the square, showrooms compete for the attention of the passers-by, all just a few steps away from busy Na Poříčí Street.

292 **UNGELT**
Týn
Old Town ①

Originally a fortified merchants' yard for custom duty collection, which is how this tiny square got its nickname – Ungelt. Granovsky Palace with its arcaded loggia and sgraffito is one of the best-preserved Renaissance gems in the city. There is a famous jazz and blues club at no. 2.

293 **AMERICKÁ/ZÁHŘEBSKÁ**
Vinohrady ④

This is not an official square, but rather an intersection of Americká and Záhřebská Streets. In the middle stands a fountain with amphibious gargoyles. Sit down on any of the terraces under the lime trees and observe the hustle and bustle of this elegant neighbourhood.

294 **MALTÉZSKÉ NÁMĚSTÍ**

Lesser Town ③

Bears the name of the Order of the Knights of Malta, who had their fortress here in the 12th century. Prick up your ears as you walk past no. 14, which is a music school for students with impaired vision. Near no. 3, sit down on Václav Havel's bench – a two-chair statue symbolising dialogue.

295 **LORETO SQUARE**

Hradčany ③

Go between 9 am and 6 pm to hear the Loreto 27-bell carillon play *A Thousand Times We Greet Thee* (every hour). Admire Chernin Palace on the opposite side of the street. Its megalomaniac proportions led to the financial ruin of the stubborn Count Chernin's. Now it's the seat of the Ministry of Foreign Affairs. The garden is open to the public.

5 *ways to*

ENJOY THE RIVER

296 **BOAT SPA**
Rašínovo nábřeží
New Town ②
+420 733 429 349
laznenalodi.cz

The winter months in Prague can be quite rough, sometimes the river even freezes. The perfect conditions to hit the boat sauna in other words. First warm up in 90°C, then jump into the river or under the shower, wrap yourself in a blanket and chill as you watch the swans glide by.

297 **RIVER CRUISE**
Between Palacký and Jirásek Bridges
Rašínovo nábřeží
New Town ②
+420 224 931 013
praguesteamboats.com

As a fitting build-up to your ZOO visit, take a steam boat from the city centre. Another option is a meander trip to Slapy Lake (south) or to the confluence of the Vltava and Elbe Rivers near Mělník (north). You receive a 10 % discount if you order your ticket online.

298 **GONDOLA CRUISE - PRAGUE VENICE**
Křížovnické náměstí 3
Old Town ①
+420 776 776 779
prague-venice.cz

Are you looking for a romantic experience, perhaps a good place for a marriage proposal or to celebrate a very special occasion? Then book a Venetian gondola cruise, which will cost you about 80 euros for half an hour. This should be just enough time to drink the champagne that comes with it.

299 PEDAL BOATS

Slovanský ostrov
New Town ②

Most rental places are located on Slovanský island, between two river weirs. A four-people boat costs 200-250 CZK for one hour, you can even select a swan or an old-timer. Proof of identity required.

300 WATER ZORBING

Slovanský ostrov
Old Town ①

Ever wanted to walk on water like Jesus? If you are willing to be zipped into a giant inflatable balloon and believe you have excellent balance skills, then try water zorbing (for 200 CZK). In many ways, it will remind you of a hamster wheel. Guaranteed to give you (or your kids) a good night's sleep.

297-299 **RIVER CRUISE-PEDAL BOATS**

The 5 loveliest
PUBLIC GARDENS

301 **FRANCISCAN GARDEN**
Jungmannovo náměstí 18
New Town ①②

Five centuries ago, Franciscan monks started growing herbs and vegetables here. Nowadays this garden is occupied by white-collar workers having lunch, bird-feeding pensioners and courting young couples. Grab a soft serve ice cream in nearby Světozor passage and enjoy the peace under the rose-laden arches.

302 **ALBERTOV BOTANIC GARDEN**
Na Slupi 16
New Town ②

The outdoor collection of this garden, which belongs to the Charles University, is free. Come here for a picnic, to read a book or stroll among the rockeries and flowerbeds. A 150-year-old ginkgo biloba grows near the greenhouse, which is home to their (sub)tropical collection.

303 **SACRÉ COEUR**
to be reached from the shopping mall or from Kartouzská Street
Smíchov ⑦

Need a quick escape from the maddening crowds in the New Smíchov shopping mall? Find the secret bridge on the first floor (near the toilets) which has a peaceful green oasis on the other side. It has several benches with a nice city view, an outdoor gym and a playground.

305 **VRTBA GARDEN**

304 VOJAN GARDENS

U Lužického semináře 17
Lesser Town ③

Just a stone's throw from the busy Charles Bridge you will find this peaceful sanctuary, which is considered the oldest partially preserved garden in Prague. Especially charming in the spring when all the fruit trees are blooming. Discover the peacock population at the back of the garden and the rose pergolas.

305 VRTBA GARDEN

Karmelitská 25
Lesser Town ③

An inconspicuous little gate guards the entrance to this UNESCO listed Baroque terrace garden. A 3-euro entrance fee buys you access to a world where Matthias Braun's statues come to life among hedge recesses and colourful floral ornaments. Climb all the stairs to enjoy a breath-taking view. Open from April till October.

5 quiet PARKS

306 **STAR GAME RESERVE**
Liboc

A walk through the former deer park in spring is particularly charming, because of the scent of the bear garlic that grows here. The summer palace in the reserve was built for feasts and to rest after the hunt. Nowadays you can still stop for refreshments here.

307 **STROMOVKA**
Bubeneč ⑨⑧

As a former royal game reserve, Stromovka boasts beautiful mature trees and a sophisticated irrigation system of canals and ponds. In the 16th century Kaiser Rudolf had a well designed and dug 45 metres below ground to supply fresh water for his game from the Vltava river.

308 **RIEGER GARDENS**
Vinohrady ④

A very popular hangout and picnic spot with the locals because of its city views. The hill near Mlíkárna bar offers the most stunning castle vistas. Bring your own drinks and if you need the public toilets after a few, then you'll find them opposite the children's playground.

309 PARUKÁŘKA
Žižkov ⑤

This hill, which overlooks the city, actually conceals an underground nuclear shelter. Built in the mid-1950s, it could accommodate up to 2500 people, generating its own electricity and with a water reservoir. Its upper plateau features a public barbecue facility, amazing views and an open-air bar.

310 KINSKI GARDEN
Náměsti Kinských
Smíchov ⑦

Originally a park surrounding the palace of this noble family, which now houses a Folklore Museum with a nice cafe terrace. There are a number of artificial grottos, a lake and a wooden orthodox church which was brought back from Western Ukraine in 1929 as a gift to the city of Prague as the country's new capital.

5

INSPIRING LIBRARIES

311 MUNICIPAL LIBRARY

Mariánské náměstí 1
Old Town ①
+420 222 113 555
mlp.cz

Open to the public for free, whether you need a peaceful place to study all day, free internet or just to use the toilet. Check their budget bistro and the endless book tunnel lined with more than 5000 volumes and some skilfully placed mirrors. Closed on Sundays and Mondays.

312 ACADEMY OF SCIENCE

Národní 3
Old Town ①
+420 221 403 208
knav.cz

The main hall of a former savings bank now is the favourite realm of bookworms. Its light and airy interior will inspire you to keep on studying. A small snack room has a tea-making facility. A one-day pass costs 10 CZK and 30 CZK with internet access.

313 NATIONAL LIBRARY

Klementinum 190
Old Town ①
+420 221 663 111
nkp.cz

A memorial building in the heart of the Old Town. The large general study hall is decorated with Baroque frescos, a collection of historic globes and a spacious courtyard. A full year's subscription will cost you 100 CZK, a one-day access card 10 CZK.

314 FACULTY OF ARTS

Náměstí J. Palacha 2
Old Town ①
+420 224 491 231
knihovna.cuni.cz

The central library of the Charles University's Faculty of Arts is situated in the cellar of the main building and is open to anyone who looks like a student. It features several study rooms and a chilling area with beanbags. For refreshments head to the student bistro, which is staffed by disabled people.

315 NATIONAL LIBRARY OF TECHNOLOGY

Technická 6
Dejvice ⑨
+420 232 002 535
techlib.cz

In the lobby print an EAN code ticket for free entry, then head to the top floor for the best view of 200 drawings that adorn the atrium's concrete walls. Only registered visitors have Wi-Fi access, but 50 CZK might be a worthy investment if you plan to stay longer.

311 MUNICIPAL LIBRARY

The 5 most

CHARMING CEMETERIES

316 **OLD JEWISH CEMETERY ŽIŽKOV**
Fibichova 2
Žižkov ⑤
synagogue.cz

Strangely enough, the second most significant Jewish cemetery in the city is squeezed between a kindergarten, a TV tower and a mini-golf course. Only part of the cemetery was preserved after 20th-century construction works.

317 **ĎÁBLICKÝ CEMETERY**
Ďáblická
Kobylisy
(tram or bus stop Sídliště Ďáblice)

This relatively young cemetery sprung up just before WW1. Once through the cubist gates you will not see any graves, which will lead you to think you entered a park. Keep walking until the ceremony hall, the grave of Heydrich's assassins or the Memory forest, where people are buried among tree roots.

318 **MADMEN'S CEMETERY**
GPS: 50.138984, 14.404582
U Drahaně
Bohnice ⑩
+420 724 028 501 (guide)

Located near a psychiatric hospital in Prague's northern suburbs. Ruins of a chapel surrounded by nameless mounds of soil covered by the omnipresent ivy commemorate around 5000 inmates buried here until the 1960s. Those of rapists and murderers are said to emit negative energy. Accessible only with a guide, Jiří Vítek.

319 OLŠANSKÉ CEMETERIES

Vinohradská 153
Žižkov ⑤
hrbitovy.cz

As Prague's largest cemetery, Olšany ballooned to 56 hectares after 300 years of use. It boasts several tomb monuments, some of which are in very bad condition. The City of Prague came up with an ingeniously cheap solution – the 'Adopt a Grave' project – allowing individuals and companies to finance their restoration.

320 MALOSTRANSKÝ CEMETERY

U Trojice 1
Smíchov ⑦
+420 722 200 908
malostranskyhrbitov.cz

This tiny cemetery was established here in 1680, near the plague hospital. Over the centuries it has managed to withstand the real estate lobbying and vandalism to reopen to the public in 2016. The combination of headless angels, fallen tombstones and ivy-covered trees is very picturesque.

320 MALOSTRANSKÝ CEMETERY

5 great examples of
ART IN PUBLIC SPACE

321 **VISELEC**
Husova 1
Old Town ①

At the top of Husova Street near Betlémské Square, you will spot a two-metre-tall bearded chap who is casually dangling from the eaves, hand in pocket. This is David Černý's depiction of (Czech-born) Sigmund Freud, symbolising the role the intellectual might play in the new millennium.

322 **ARTWALL GALLERY**
Nábřeží Kapitána Jaroše
Holešovice ⑧
+420 731 512 512
artwallgallery.cz

This wall, which originally served as a space for communist propaganda, now aims to support the social impact of contemporary art in a non-gallery environment. The left embankment along the Vltava regularly comes alive with photo exhibitions, which often are a source of controversy.

323 MEMENTO MORI

Folimanka Park
Vinohrady ④

Once in the park, make your way under the high Nusle Bridge to look for this unusual sculpture by Krištof Kintera. This warped lamp post is a memento to all those who committed suicide by diving into the valley. Since its construction in 1973, between two and three hundred people have ended their lives here.

324 BRONZE HORSES

Crossing of Kafkova and Kyjevská Streets
Dejvice ⑨

A herd of bronze horses has fluttered into a river fountain in a small square in front of the Hus Congregational House. The sculptor Michal Gabriel chose the motif to reflect on these noble creatures, who once trotted where cars now run. This place is very popular with children on a hot summer's day.

325 LETNÁ TUNNEL

Kostelní/Muzejní
Holešovice ⑧

In a park right behind the National Technical Museum two strange chimneys rise up towards the sky. Although they have a specific practical function, namely providing ventilation for the underground Letná tunnel, they look like a unique work of art because of the beautiful timeless black and white mosaic by Zdeněk Sýkora.

323 **MEMENTO MORI**

5 of the most
MYSTICAL PLACES

326 **SAINT VITUS AT SUMMER SOLSTICE**
Křížovnické náměstí
Old Town ①③

During the summer solstice, you can observe something quite spectacular from a square next to the Charles Bridge. The last sunrays of the day illuminate the Golden Gate Tower, the oldest part of Saint Vitus Cathedral, where the remains of the Czech patron saint are buried.

327 **SAINT MARY COLUMN**
Old Town Square
Old Town ①

Only five square tiles remind us today where Saint Mary's Column once stood. It was built out of gratitude because the people felt that she had protected the city during the Thirty Years' War, and marked a spiritual centre of Europe. It was unceremoniously knocked down in autumn 1918 as a symbol of Habsburg dominion. Saint Mary's statue stands near the right wall of Týn Dome.

328 **VYŠEHRAD**
②

No place can be more mystical in Prague than Vyšehrad, which is shrouded in legend and history. The first Czech Royal Dynasty was founded by Princess Libuše on this rocky promontory above the Vltava River. She uttered a prophecy about the location where she saw 'a great city whose glory will touch the stars'. You can also find the Slavín Mausoleum and the Devil's Column within the fortress.

329 **PRAGUE'S GEOPUNCTURE**

Litopuncture – or acupuncture for landscape – is a project of the Slovenian sculptor Marko Pogacnik, who installed several stone menhirs with bronze symbols in various locations in Prague. Prague's heart axis extends from Strahov monastery, to Hlavní nádraží tram station, and ends in Parukářka Park.

330 **ROTUNDA OF THE FINDING OF THE HOLY CROSS**
Karolíny Světlé
Old Town ①

A Romanesque rotunda, the oldest sacred place in Prague. It was already here before the Old Town was developed, built from opuka on the original level of the land which was later elevated due to flooding. The Old Catholic Church maintains the premises and holds evening prayers on Sundays, Tuesdays and Fridays.

STUDIO ALTA

45 PLACES TO ENJOY CULTURE

5 galleries to discover
NEW TALENT

331 **FINE ARTS ACADEMY**
U Akademie 4
Bubeneč ⑧
+420 220 408 224
avu.cz

The tiny gallery on the first floor is open to the public. Roam around its corridors, cluttered with plaster experiments, take a peek in the studios through open doors. Then walk downstairs to the backgarden to admire the baroque statues in the grass and the building's beautiful terraced façade.

332 **TRAFO GALLERY**
Bubenské nábřeží 13
Holešovice ⑧
+420 739 517 758
trafacka.cz

Market halls 14 and 18 became the new home of this gallery, after it was evicted from an old convertor station in Vysočany. It continues to present Czech artists against a bizarre backdrop of Chinese goods and became a valuable addition to the increasingly famous Artdistrict 7.

333 **GALERIE DRDOVA**
Křížkovského 10
Žižkov ⑤
+420 777 216 416
drdovagallery.com

Located in an upscale residential part of Žižkov district, just around the corner from the TV tower. In a series of ground-floor rooms, Lucie Drdová curates the works of a dozen Czech, Slovak and Slovenian artists who permanently live in the country.

334 GALERIE JELENÍ

Dukelských hrdinů 25a
Holešovice ⑧
+420 222 986 116
cca.fcca.cz

This forgotten courtyard in Holešovice used to be a bakery. Now it is owned by the Prague Centre for Contemporary Arts and supports young emerging artists who often have their first solo exhibition here. Occasionally work by older but influential artists is shown here, too.

335 NOD GALLERY

Dlouhá 33
Old Town ①
+420 773 252 673
nod.roxy.cz

Located above a legendary music club, the NoD experimental multi-genre space is its more alternative sibling. The gallery presents the latest trends and experimental tendencies in contemporary art in cooperation with young up-and-coming talent on the art scene.

The 5 best places to admire MODERN AND CONTEMPORARY ART

336 **MEET FACTORY**
Ke Sklárně 15
Smíchov ⑦
+420 251 551 796
www.meetfactory.cz

This international art centre and residence can be found in between the railway and a busy road. The building's industrial origin was perfectly suited for creating a minimalistic platform that combines different art genres, from the visual arts to music and cinema. In its central bar, you are sure to bump into a Bohemian.

337 **DOX**
Poupětova 1
Holešovice ⑧
+420 295 568 123
dox.cz

Roughly the size of a football pitch, DOX gallery showcases contemporary art. Its name derives from the Greek word doxa, or a way of perceiving things. Art projects that also include a critical reflection on current social issues. Everyone is entitled to their opinion here. Recently a zeppelin called Gulliver parked on the roof.

338 **STONE BELL HOUSE**
Staroměstské náměstí 13
Old Town ①
+420 224 826 391
ghmp.cz

Near the Old Town Square stands a unique, preserved house, an exceptional example of Gothic tower palace architecture. It is now a municipal gallery that hosts contemporary exhibitions on its three floors. Art within art.

337 DOX

DOX
ART
IS WHAT
MAKES
LIFE MORE
INTERESTING
THAN ART.
RISK!
RISK
ANYTHING!
FACE THE TRUTH.
ACT FOR YOURSELF.
THE TRAGEDY OF MODERN MAN
THE MEANING OF HIS OWN LIFE,
NOTHING TO DO WITH POLITICS
LIVING AT RISK IS JUMPING
OFF THE CLIFF AND

339 **TRADE FAIR PALACE**
Dukelských hrdinů 47
Holešovice ⑧
+420 224 301 122
ngprague.cz

This Functionalist architectural gem houses (inter)national art from the 19th century onwards, including works by Picasso, Klimt and Mucha. During WWII, people were rounded up here before leaving for concentration camps. It has a trendy cafe on the ground floor. A ticket entitles you to visit all other permanent exhibitions in the National Gallery within a week.

340 **KAMPA MUSEUM**
U Sovových mlýnů 2
Lesser Town ③
+420 257 286 147
museumkampa.com

Meda Mládek will soon celebrate her 100th birthday and what an exceptional life she has lived. A passionate art collector who lives mostly abroad, she has been a committed promoter of František Kupka and even sold the family house to buy his paintings. In Sova Mills she exhibits the largest private collection of work by Kupka in the world.

5 hidden INDEPENDENT CINEMAS

341 **BIO OKO**
Františka Křížka 15
Holešovice ⑧
+420 608 33 00 88
biooko.net

Bio Oko is one of the reasons why Veverkova Street has become so fashionable lately. This cinema with a stylish bar and craft brews on tap hosts film brunches on Sundays from 10 am till 12 noon. Can you think of a better start to a lazy day?

342 **KINO DLABAČOV**
Bělohorská 24
Břevnov ③
+420 233 102 991
dlabacov.cz

Situated in the eye-catching Pyramid Hotel, this tiny cinema has come back to life after decades. It offers a good mix of popular films and world cinema, matinées for pensioners, special screenings for kids and stand-up comedy for parents. The cafe with a playground corner is an added bonus.

343 **PONREPO**
Bartolomějská 11
Old Town ①
+420 778 522 708
nfa.cz

You can find the cinema of the National Film Archives in a former boarding school refectory. Its 150 million-metre-long collection is considered one of the world's ten largest collections. As its mission is to protect and promote cinematic heritage, it mostly shows older and lesser known movies. There are two screenings every evening.

344 **KINO AERO**

Biskupcova 31
Žižkov ⑤
+420 271 771 349
kinoaero.cz

Žižkov has plenty of courtyards, but only one of them is home to a tiny cinema. Visit in March for the Shockproof Film Festival – if you dare – or at any other time of the year to drink your pint or Kofola while watching one of their eclectic world movies. Head for the middle row and emergency exit row, which has extra legroom.

345 **KINO PILOTŮ**

Donská 19
Vršovice ④
+420 723 985 986
kinopilotu.cz

This recently renovated small cinema has just two theatres, which show up to fourteen movies a day, focusing on alternative films in their subtitled original versions. For a truly unforgettable experience book the virtual reality room which is crammed with high-tech gadgets.

344 KINO AERO

The 5 best

FESTIVALS TO VISIT

346 **OPEN HOUSE PRAGUE**
MAY
openhousespraha.cz

In 2015, Prague joined European and American cities in the Open Houses festival of architecture. For one week, usually inaccessible buildings open their doors to the public, which has been flocking to the festival in ever larger droves. Interested in the PM seat or the HBO headquarters? Visits are free but booking in advance is recommended.

347 **UNITED ISLANDS OF PRAGUE**
JUNE
unitedislands.cz

This event brings a different genre to each island, along the river and in nearby gardens. Discover Czech rap, a drummer ensemble of disabled musicians or Israeli jazz. Special awesomeness factor: can you think of any other music festival where you can take a ferry or a pedal boat to get from one stage to another?

348 **SUMMER LETNÁ**
AUGUST/SEPTEMBER
letniletna.cz

Since 2004, this festival has transformed the Letná plateau into immense circus grounds. Over the years it has become a world-renowned institution, presenting the work of contemporary circus and theatre companies to the general public. Sip a beer under the trees as you watch their acrobatic creations.

349 **DIFFERENT CITY EXPERIENCE**
SEPTEMBER
zazitmestojinak.cz

This festival is organised as part of the European Week of Mobility, which aims to promote sustainable means of urban development. It focuses on reclaiming public space and community building. Experience a different side of the city with lively streets full of music, joy and smiling people.

350 **DESIGN BLOK**
OCTOBER
designblok.cz

The most important event for all design freaks. Since 1999, it has presented a selection of items from all over Europe, including new prestigious brands and prototypes of emerging as well as already established designers and studios. Attracts over 50.000 visitors every year.

The 5 coolest
MUSIC CLUBS

351 **GROOVE BAR**
Voršilská 6
New Town ②
+420 777 610 279
groovebar.cz

One of those rare places where you can listen to deep house and techno music in Prague. The club is smallish, but always lively with a vibrant atmosphere. Throw in some nice staff, reasonably priced drinks and you can see why it is such a favourite.

352 **AKROPOLIS**
Kubelíkova 27
Žižkov ⑤
+420 296 330 913
palacakropolis.cz

Akropolis is a temple to alternative culture, including music, theatre and performance. The interior features quirky metalwork pieces, which will catch your attention as soon as you enter the foyer. Here they do not distinguish between emerging local names and foreign stars, as long as they rock. Or soul. Or hip-hop.

353 **KLUB 007**
Chaloupeckého 7
Břevnov ③
+420 775 260 071
klub007strahov.cz

An underground (literally) club in one of the student accommodation blocks on top of Petřín Hill. Since 1969, they host local as well as international bands in all genres, from punk to rockabilly and from sub pop to noise.

354 **KLUBOVNA 2. PATRO**
Dlouhá 37
Old Town ①

After passing through a magnificent, shabby chic courtyard with late-Renaissance arcades, turn left and climb up to the second floor. Here you will find a large hall where the first Prague computer once stood. It took up the entire space and had the capacity of a pocket calculator. Since then, it made way for an improvised gallery, punk theatre and most importantly, a club hosting awesome DJ sets.

355 **ROXY**
Dlouhá 33
Old Town ①
roxy.cz

Roxy is one of the biggest and longest standing music clubs in Prague. This former Art Deco movie theatre has an impressive L-Acoustics sound system for top notch sound quality. A wide range of artists have already performed here, including DJ Shadow or Mogwai.

355 ROXY

5 alternative
CULTURAL CENTRES

356 **KLUBOVNA**
Generála Píky
Dejvice ⑨
+420 739 834 056
klubovna.povalec.cz

As a cultural and community centre, Klubovna hosts concerts of young Prague bands and international guests, regular film and theatre evenings, lectures, debates as well as very popular haircut sessions. A shady garden, sauna and a community compost pile are a welcome bonus.

357 **ŠKOLSKÁ 28**
Školská 28
New Town ②
+420 222 966 974
skolska28.cz

Tucked away in a spacious courtyard, this space primarily focuses on international cultural dialogue, through multidisciplinary artistic and educational activities. They regularly host exhibitions, music improv performances, art installations and festivals with subjects ranging from performance art, sound or video art to electronic music.

358 **STUDIO ALTA**
U Výstaviště 21
Holešovice ⑧
altart.cz

In four industrial halls with a floor area of almost 1800 sq m, Alta is a multicultural centre that focuses on contemporary dance. There are two theatres, various workshops (including for children) and a cosy cafe guarded by a local Dude Cat. Utterly delightful.

358 **STUDIO ALTA**

359 **JATKA 78**

359 **JATKA 78**
Bubenské nábřeží 13
Holešovice ⑧
+420 773 134 884
jatka78.cz

After the recent opening of this haven of creativity in halls 7 and 8 in the city market grounds, this has become an icon of Holešovice and its varied cultural scene. The residence of three of Prague's new circus companies, it welcomes international acrobats as well.

360 **TOVÁRNA**
Dělnická 63
Holešovice ⑧

An incubator for various skilled people such as passionate (motor) bikers, creative artists, progressive filmmakers or great bartenders. This place clearly doesn't believe in labels. This former industrial building has been transformed into a public platform for creativity. Come for a workshop, visit the flea market or just check out the cafe.

The 5 most interesting
TRADITIONAL MUSEUMS

361 **CONVENT OF ST AGNES OF BOHEMIA**
U Milosrdných 17
Old Town ①
+420 778 725 086
ngprague.cz

These walls take you right back to the Middle Ages. No wonder then that this part of the National Gallery focuses on that period. If you tire of admiring Madonnas and gilded saints, then check out the outdoor sculpture exhibition or chill in the convent gardens. You don't need a ticket to visit them.

362 **LANGWEIL'S MODEL OF PRAGUE**
AT: CITY OF PRAGUE MUSEUM
Na Poříčí 52
Karlín ⑥
+420 221 012 911
muzeumprahy.cz

On the second floor of the city museum you can see a unique 18th-century paper model of Prague. Thanks to a recent digitisation you can now explore over 2000 buildings, half of which no longer exist. This realistic model covers a floor area of 20 sq m and took Antonín Langweil eleven years to build.

363 **TRABANT MUSEUM**
Plzeňská 215
Motol
+420 725 555 149
trabantmuzeum.cz

The founder's mum was a passionate car racer, who fell in love with Trabis in the 1960s. For decades, people in the Eastern zone went on holiday in this super-light vehicle (with a body made of duroplast, a cotton-based water resistant material). Or at least the lucky ones – the waiting lists were up to 30 years long!

364 TROJA CHATEAU

U Trojského zámku 1
Troja ⑩
+420 283 851 614
ghmp.cz/zamek-troja

This magnificent building stands in the middle of a beautiful French landscape garden with a hedge maze. Built in the late 18th century, the frescos in the main hall reflect the Baroque splendour of its Italianate inspiration. It belongs to the city gallery, which regularly hosts temporary exhibitions and concerts here.

365 NATIONAL TECHNICAL MUSEUM

Kostelní 42
Holešovice ⑧
+420 220 399 111
ntm.cz

This six-floor building stands on the Letná plateau and has 14 permanent thematic exhibitions, from architecture to astronomy and the measurement of time to the technology of toys. You can see Charlie Chaplin's hat, an impressive collection of vehicles or the Czech Expo 1958 fountain. Expect to spend a few hours here.

363 TRABANT MUSEUM

5 significant places for BOHUMIL HRABAL

366 **NA HRÁZI 24**
Libeň

Number 24, where Hrabal spent more than 20 years in a stale-smelling studio, was demolished to build a metro station. A commemorative wall covered with his texts, cats and books reminds passers-by how much he loved the peripheric poetry of Libeň.

367 **PALÁC SVĚT**
Elsnicovo náměstí 6
Libeň

This palace, which was built in 1930, has preserved very little of it former glory. In its heyday, it was a lively place with a cinema, a cafe and a gambling club, all of which Hrabal regularly visited with his friends. He set his collection of short stories, called *The World Cafetaria*, here.

368 **AT THE GOLDEN TIGER**
Husova 17
Old Town ①
+420 222 221 111
uzlatehotygra.cz

A humble pub in which Hrabal held court and granted private audiences to important political figures, such as Václav Havel or Bill Clinton. This was where he distributed his samizdat works, which were banned by the regime. Unlike most places downtown, this one somehow managed to retain its character.

369 HOTEL PARIS

U Obecního domu 1
Old Town ①
+420 222 195 195
hotel-paris.cz

It was here that Hrabal's character Jan Dítě honed his skills of perception under the watchful tutelage of the headwaiter Mr Skrivanek, who served the King of England in the eponymous novel. Later Dítě would wait on the Emperor of Ethiopia, receiving a medal about which he brags.

370 NA BULOVCE HOSPITAL

Budínova 2
Libeň

Hrabal died here at the age of 83 after a fall from the third floor, allegedly while feeding pigeons. A hint of mystery surrounds his death, all the more so given the frequent appearance of suicide in his works. Living a joyless life means 'you must find the courage to wrap it up', he used to say...

366 NA HRÁZI 24

5 significant places for FRANZ KAFKA

371 **FRANZ KAFKA'S BIRTH HOUSE**
Náměstí Franze Kafky
Old Town ①

A bronze bust reminds passers-by that Franz Kafka was born here on 3 July 1883 as the first child of his parents. The Kafkas moved quite often, but always within the confines of the Old Town Jewish ghetto and within walking distance to the Synagogue. Only the Baroque gate survived after the slums of Josefov were cleared.

372 **WORKERS' ACCIDENT INSURANCE INSTITUTE**
Na Poříčí 7
New Town ①

Kafka worked in this building (now a hotel) as a clerk for 14 years until his retirement in 1922. He found his daily duties rather tedious, he often came to work extremely tired after spending the whole night writing.

373 **MUSEUM**
Cihelná 2
Lesser Town ③
+420 257 535 507
kafkamuseum.cz

This captivating museum contains a linear journey through Kafka's life, which is documented with photographs, letters, diaries, manuscripts and first editions of his works. Intriguing 3D installations and audiovisual pieces also shed light on his inspiration, deepest fears and wildest thoughts.

374 METALMORPHOSIS

Spálená 22
New Town ②

A moveable stainless steel statue in the form of Kafka's head. This 39-ton giant is the work of David Černý, a controversial local artist who is infamous for his statue guerilla. Forty-two layers are programmed to perform a 40-minute-long choreography and attract the attention of passers-by.

375 NEW JEWISH CEMETERY

Izrealská 1
Žižkov ⑤

After a long struggle, Kafka finally succumbed to tuberculosis one month before his 41st birthday. He was buried in a family grave under a Cubist tombstone about 200 metres from the entrance. A plaque opposite commemorates Max Brod, Kafka's dear friend who refused to burn all his manuscripts after his death as instructed.

374 METALMORPHOSIS

HUGO CHODÍ BOS

25 THINGS TO DO WITH CHILDREN

5 *child-friendly* RESTAURANTS AND CAFES

376 **DIVOKÉ MATKY**
Hybešova 2
Karlín ⑥
+420 607 022 899
divokakavarna.wixsite.com/kavarna

Hipster mum HQ. Founded by three friends who are dancers-actors and who refused to feel lonely as young mums. Organises workshops for kids and serves excellent coffee. The only risk is that your children might not want to leave.

377 **KAVÁRNA MALUJ**
Korunní 98
Vinohrady ④
+420 774 625 851
www.kavarnamaluj.cz

This creative cafe, which is conveniently located close to Náměstí Míru, teaches your offspring (and you) to become pottery painters. They offer several courses including pottery making and mosaic building. The teachers are fluent in English and international groups are welcome.

378 **VOZOVNA**
Královská obora 2
Bubeneč ⑧
+420 725 123 705
vozovna-stromovka.cz

This restaurant in a refurbished tram depot is located in the very heart of the former Royal Game Reserve. The adjacent outdoor playground will please smaller children with its play train, the older crowd will love the rope glider. The menu includes several kid-friendly options. Cash payment only.

379 **KRÁLÍK V RÁDIU**
Křižíkova 65a
Karlín ⑥
+420 732 428 929
kralikvradiu.cz

This cafe cropped up in the aftermath of the heyday of the Krymská neighbourhood, then moved to Karlín. As Hippie/sters became older, they had babies and refused to feel lonely at home. They have a playroom with every toy imaginable and a group babysitter so parents can run their errands (120 CZK per hour – three hours maximum).

380 **KOALA KAFÉ**
Dolnoměcholupská 17
Hostivař
+420 212 241 171
koalakafe.cz

A perfect place for a kid's birthday party or on a rainy afternoon. Located in the former film studios, this cafe has a gigantic playground with slides and jungle gyms for all ages. And of course, it wouldn't be complete without a ball pit. Hours of Zzzz guaranteed after your visit.

The 5 best shops to buy
TOYS

381 **HUGO CHODÍ BOS**
Řeznická 12
New Town ②
+420 602 834 930
hugochodibos.cz

This nostalgic wooden toy store was founded as an alternative to the plastic toys from Asia that flood the market. Adéla H. Kantůrková started to tour the country to find Czech-made pieces that were certified, environmentally friendly and develop children's creativity.

382 **YOYO STORE**
V Jirchářích 12
New Town ②
+420 732 547 377
www.yoyostore.cz

A place for older children and anyone who refuses to grow up. Here they will find an impressive range of yoyos, frisbees, discgolf accessories, kendamas and other skill toys. Lessons are organised twice a week for those who want to learn and improve their skills.

383 **OOKIDOO**
Ostrovní 21
New Town ②
+420 723 013 012
www.ookidoo.com

Here you can shop for high-quality creative toys from all four corners of the earth. Looking for large puzzles for little hands, colourful playshapes or environmentally friendly rubberwood building kits? No need to search any longer, they probably have it here or in their e-shop.

384 **HRAČKOTÉKA**
Školská 34
New Town ②
+420 222 965 565
hrackoteka.cz

After having children, Jana and Barbora felt there was a shortage of creative and educational toys, so they imported them from the Low Countries, Denmark and France. They started out as an e-shop but then decided to build a store and hire employees with disabilities. A wide selection of items for toddlers, creative sets for older children, as well as artistic workshops.

385 **DŘEVĚNÝ SVĚT HRAČEK**
Francouzská 110
Vršovice ④
+420 606 121 833
drevenysvethracek.cz

A simple wooden toy store outside the city centre, not as glamorous as the other ones on this list but with a wide selection of reasonably priced items. They sell building sets, abacuses, puppets and popular cartoon characters, such as the Little Mole.

381 HUGO CHODÍ BOS

5 places to

OBSERVE WILDLIFE

386 **BIRDS ON THE RIVER**
Smíchovská náplavka
Smíchov ⑦

The sandy area near the railway bridge was once called Prague Beach. Human visitors, however, did not appreciate the city's efforts as much as its winged ones. This part of the left bank is the calmest one. Here you will see large flocks of resting swans, geese, gulls and pigeons.

387 **MOUFLONS IN A HOSPITAL**
Kunratice Forest and Thomayer Hospital

A hospital surrounded by woods. In fact, it even used to have a fence around it. Then nosy mouflons found loopholes and started paying visits to local patients who generously fed them. The hospital's management acknowledge the positive effects of such animal therapy and turn a blind eye on the four-legged trespassers.

388 **NUTRIA COLONY**
Hloubětín

Take a stroll along a small creek called Rokytka, which became home to a large colony of nutrias. Some complain about these invasive species, but most people like to watch them emerge from the holes dug in the riverbanks, swim around and wait to be fed vegetables.

389 **CROCODILE ZOO**

Tusarova 39
Holešovice ⑧
+420 728 492 488
krokodylipraha.cz

How old are modern crocodiles? How large are the largest and the smallest ones? What is their body temperature? The perfect place to ask any questions you ever wanted to ask. If you can bear it, come at 10.30 am or 2 pm during the weekend to watch the feeding frenzy.

390 **CLUB OF YOUNG NATURAL SCIENTISTS**

Drtinova 1a
Smíchov ⑦
+420 222 333 860
ddmpraha.cz/stanice-prirodovedcu

Children will love the playground. You can pet ponies and a Cameroon goat or explore outdoor aviaries with kangaroos, parrots, and a marten. There is also a tropical terrarium, an ecologically-oriented nature trail, a geological exposition and a herb garden.

The 5 best spots for a FUN PICNIC

391 **RADOTÍNSKO – CHUCHELSKÝ HÁJ**
V Lázních
Malá Chuchle

This upstream forest park has everything you need to keep you busy all day: a quarry with a nearby barbecue spot, a lovely meadow with jungle gyms, a slide and a sandbox. There is a ZOO corner nearby, where wounded forest animals are nursed back to health.

392 **PŘÍSTAV 18600**
GPS: 50.096330, 14.448062
Karlín ⑥
+420 728 550 984
18600.cz

A community project to successfully revive the Karlín riverbank from May till October. A bar, playgrounds, a beach volleyball pitch, barbecue rental, regular DJ sets, concerts and performances make this a perfect hip family place. For more fun take the ferry from Holešovice.

393 **RAJSKÁ ZAHRADA**
U Rajské zahrady
Žižkov ⑤

The garden of this former vineyard has a huge playground with a friendly cafe, ping-pong tables, slides and (jungle) gyms. The gloriette is perched atop a staircase with a water cascade. This Paradise Garden is very popular with young mums and young lovers from the nearby University of Economics.

394 PARK PODVINNÍ

Rubeška 5
Vysočany

Perched on the right bank of Rokytka creek, the most striking part of this park is a (fake) Celtic settlement with corridors and tunnels overlooking Dragon Lake. It also has a rope park, an amphitheatre and several small ponds with lush vegetation. Definitely check out the playground.

395 PARK & CASTLE PRŮHONICE

Zámek 1
Průhonice
+420 271 015 211
parkpruhonice.cz
pruhonickypark.cz

Situated in the south-east, on the outskirts of Prague, but easy to get to by public transport, Průhonice park is a real gem and worth the journey. Set around an exquisite castle (not accessible to the public) this lovely landscape park is home to the largest collection of rhododendrons. It even made it onto the UNESCO heritage list.

392 PŘÍSTAV 18600

5 activities for a RAINY DAY

396 **DIVADLO MINOR**
Vodičkova 6
New Town ②
+420 222 231 351
minor.cz

A mesmerising kids' theatre called Minor. They stage a wide range of plays for kids of all ages. Backstage visits are also possible. And don't forget to check out the playing gallery and the cafe.

397 **PLANETÁRIUM**
Královská obora 233
Bubeneč ⑧
+420 220 999 001
planetarium.cz

Choose one of the three English shows on offer (the others are in Czech), lean back in your comfy seat and enjoy the projection on one of the world's biggest spherical domes. The foyer hosts temporary exhibitions on space related topics, such as astronomy or time.

398 **KAREL ZEMAN MUSEUM**
Saská 3
Lesser Town ③
+420 724 341 091
muzeumkarlazemana.cz

Karel Zeman, sometimes nicknamed 'Czech Méliès', was a film director, who combined live-action footage with animation. Here you can discover his fantasy world, take a ride on a flying machine, walk on the moon like Baron Munchausen, or sit at the controls of the famous submarine from *The Fabulous World of Jules Verne.*

399 ARTPARK RUDOLFINUM

Alšovo nábřeží 12
Old Town ①
+420 770 100 767
galerierudolfinum.cz

Artpark presents the past and present of art in an accessible way. This interactive guide to contemporary art is more suited to older children and teenagers. What is art? What are all the possible meanings of an ordinary apple? Let them find the answers.

400 MUNICIPAL PUBLIC TRANSPORT MUSEUM

Patočkova 4
Střešovice ③
+420 296 128 900
dpp.cz/en/urban-mass-transit-museum

What kind of trams did our ancestors used to commute? What was it like to drive them? When did the first metro set run? The Museum is housed in a listed depot monument and has an extensive collection of models and vehicles, as well as interesting timetables, tickets and drawings.

ONE ROOM HOTEL

20 PLACES TO SLEEP

The 5 best

BOUTIQUE HOTELS

401 U RAKA HOUSE

Černínská 10
Hradčany ③
+420 220 511 100
hoteluraka.cz

Most people would expect to find a typical timbered country house like this one on the slopes of the Giant Mountains instead of near Prague Castle. This small romantic hotel has an enchanting private garden, a fireplace and a charming cafe so you always enjoy a warm welcome.

402 BOTEL KLOTYLDA

Masarykovo nábřeží
New Town ②
+420 222 511 826
botelmatylda.cz

This stylish boat hotel is moored halfway between Prague's two castles, with ancient Šítkovská Tower on one side and the modern Dancing House on the other. It has 25 rooms, a third of which are located on the neighbouring Matylda boat, which also has a restaurant on board.

403 VILA LANNA

V Sadech 1
Bubeneč ⑨
+420 224 321 278
data.vila-lanna.ssc.avcr.cz

This neo-Renaissance landmark building is situated near the Royal Game Reserve and was the summer retreat of a prominent nouveau-riche. Very little has changed here since the end of the 19th century, except perhaps that it is now also a conference and wedding venue.

404 MISS SOPHIE'S

Melounova 3
New Town ②
+420 246 032 620
miss-sophies.com

A modern, cosy hotel in a 19th-century Art Nouveau building. The perfect base for exploring New Town and Vinohrady. They have a kitchen for guests, but you might not need it as they serve a copious all-you-can-eat breakfast buffet.

405 HOTEL JALTA

Václavské náměstí 45
New Town ②
+420 222 822 111
hoteljalta.com

A prime example of Socialist Realism. Hotel Jalta was where foreign news correspondents stayed during the Communist era and was infamous because its rooms were bugged by the secret police. The fallout shelter under the hotel now houses a Cold War Museum. Still a glamorous hotel in a very central location.

401 U RAKA HOUSE

5 of the hippest
DESIGN HOTELS

406 HOTEL SAX

Jánský vršek 3
Lesser Town ③
+420 257 531 268
hotelsax.cz

This vintage design hotel is tucked away in the quaint streets under Petřín Hill, next to the mysterious Museum of Alchemists and Magicians. It combines a central location with a peaceful setting. From the hotel's fourth-floor terraces, you can enjoy magnificent views of the Castle and Lesser Town rooftops.

407 NYX HOTEL

Panská 9
New Town ①
+420 226 222 800
nyx-hotels.com/prague

A former bank by the prominent 20th-century architect Jan Gočár has since been transformed into a hotel. Paying tribute to his style, it combines modern simplicity with street art in the lobby and rooms, which were designed by various young Czech designers. Very centrally-located near bustling Wenceslas Square.

408 HOTEL BOHO

Senovážná 4
New Town ①
+420 234 622 600
hotelbohoprague.com

Walk through the imposing lobby to your elegant, beautifully-appointed room with natural shades and materials. When you see the luxurious wellness areas, you might even refuse to ever leave the hotel. Which would be a shame, as it has a fantastic location for exploring the Old Town.

409 HOTEL JOSEF

Rybná 20
Old Town ①
+420 221 700 901
hoteljosef.com

This gem of modernist architecture was ingeniously built into the existing historical building complex. Its bright and airy lobby was designed by a world-renowned architect of Czech origin, Eva Jiřičná. Besides comfortable rooms, the hotel also has its own bakery, so expect warm crusty bread for breakfast.

410 MOODS BOUTIQUE HOTEL

Klimentská 28
New Town ①
+420 222 330 100
www.hotelmoods.com

Marvel at this hotel's amazing design scheme, behind its historical façade, with unusual natural materials, Artemide lighting and Hästens beds. This award-winning project by two design students allows guests to adapt the space according to their own mood. Control the lights, music and other elements in the room with an iPhone.

5 lodgings for a ROOM WITH A VIEW

411 ONE ROOM HOTEL

Mahlerovy sady 1
Žižkov ⑤
+420 210 320 085
towerpark.cz/en/hotel+4

As its name suggests, this hotel has limited availability. Nestled 70 metres above the ground in the TV tower, this room simply has one of the best views in Prague. It's up to you to decide whether a package including a romantic dinner plus the services of a personal butler and driver is worth almost 1000 euros.

412 MOSAIC HOUSE

Odborů 4
New Town ②
+420 221 595 350
mosaichouse.com

A lodge designed by eco-pioneers who take pride in being the first Prague zero emission hotel. Their top floor penthouses have superb views of the Castle and Prague's rooftops. Downstairs they have their own music club, which hosts concerts or karaoke events.

413 AUGUSTINE HOTEL

Letenská 12
Lesser Town ③
+420 266 112 233
augustinehotel.com

One of Prague's best hotels, located in the grounds of a former monastery. Its rooms have vaulted ceilings, wooden beams or original doors with ornamental ironwork. All the marble mosaic bathrooms have heated floors. You will have the entire city at your feet in the Tower Suite.

414 DANCING HOUSE HOTEL

Jiráskovo náměstí 6
New Town ②
+420 720 983 172
dancinghousehotel.com

Since its construction, the Dancing House splits public opinion between those who despise modern elements in the old city centre and those who adore this architectural tribute to Ginger Rogers and Fred Astaire. The rooms in Ginger's skirt offer a panoramic view of the Castle and National Theatre, which towers over the river.

415 HOTEL GOLDEN STAR

Nerudova 48
Lesser Town ③
+420 257 532 867
hotelgoldenstar.cz

Situated near the Castle gate, this contemporary hotel contrasts sharply with its picturesque surroundings. Minimalist rooms accentuate period features. The hearty breakfast and its great location make this a winning combination, from where you can discover the most charming spots before the crowds flock in.

411 ONE ROOM HOTEL

The 5 nicest
HOSTELS

416 **HOSTEL SOKOL**
Nosticova 2
Lesser Town ③
+420 257 007 397
sokol.eu/obsah/5391/hostel-sokol

You won't find any other 12-euro accommodation in the heart of the Lesser Town, just a stone's throw away from the Charles Bridge. Located within the headquarters of the Czech Republic's largest sport association called Sokol, it offers basic but clean dorms and a few double rooms. Check out the rooftop terrace and the pool.

417 **HOSTEL BOUDNÍK**
Dalimilova 4
Žižkov ⑤
+420 776 578 736
hostelboudnik.com

Žižkov district has the highest number of bars per square metre, making it the perfect destination for party people. Large, comfortable rooms with a 1960s décor and a homely feel, within walking distance from the main bus terminal.

418 **AHOY! HOSTEL**
Na Perštýně 10
Old Town ①
+420 773 004 003
ahoyhostel.com

It hardly gets more central than this place, between the Old Town Square and Národní. Located in a 17th-century building, near famous monuments, with Prague's wild nightlife right on the doorstep it ticks all the boxes for most young travellers.

419 SIR TOBY'S HOSTEL

Dělnická 24
Holešovice ⑧
+420 246 032 611
sirtobys.com

Fifteen years ago, Mathias Schwender was inspired to open a hostel in this neighbourhood, long before it became hip and arty. The tourist hotspots are just a short tram ride away, but there are plenty of local hangouts to investigate nearby. Retro furnishings, a bar in the cellar and a garden for BBQs.

420 POST HOSTEL

Moravská 9
Vinohrady ④
+420 702 158 270
posthostelprague.com

Stylish modern accommodation in the heart of an elegant residential quarter, which makes it a very good deal, starting at €10 a night. The hostel shares a building with the post office (remember to send your postcards), has spacious light rooms with double-height ceilings and a game room.

419 SIR TOBY'S HOSTEL

SEMINARY GARDEN

40 ACTIVITIES FOR WEEKENDS

The 5 most beautiful

WALKS IN THE WOODS

421 **PROKOPSKÉ VALLEY**
(bus or train to Nádraží Hlubočepy)

A valley lined with rocks, quarries and caves in the south-western suburbs. A 6-kilometre yellow track starts near the Barrandov-Geologická tram stop and winds its way to metro Jinonice. If you don't feel like walking, then take the Prague Semmering train, which leaves four times a day from Prague's Main Train Station.

422 **DIVOKÁ ŠÁRKA**
(Divoká Šárka tram stop)

This valley and gorge located en route to the airport will take your breath away. A red tourist footpath from the tram terminus will guide you to a swimming pool guaranteeing a refreshing dip, supplied by clean fresh water from the Šárecký creek. You can walk or cycle along it for 8 more kilometres.

423 NATURAL PARK KOŠÍŘE-MOTOL

(Poštovka tram stop or U Lesíka bus stop)

This 20-hectare nature reserve comprises Cibulka Park and was established in 1815 on former farmland. It has a Chinese Pavilion and a romantic belvedere, which is perfect for admiring the sunset. Across the train tracks, you can see Vidoule table mountain and its many pure water springs.

424 POŽÁRY QUARRY

(train to Řeporyje or bus Řeporyjské náměstí)

Explore the slopes, rocky outposts and walls of this abandoned flooded limestone quarry, which was formed by rocky forests about 400 million years old. Just off the main route you can find a narrow-gauge tunnel that was built in 1930 for limestone transports from Požáry.

425 NATURAL PARK DRAHÁŇ-TROJA

(Podhoří or Zámky bus stops, train to Sedlec and then ferry)

⑩

This nature park extends along the River Vltava in Prague's suburbs. It is located near the ZOO and is best explored by bike or on roller skates. From Drahaňské údolí a blue path will take you back to a bus. Otherwise the route continues further north to Klecánky and Kralupy, all the way to the confluence with the Elbe River.

5

RIVER ISLANDS

to discover

426 **STŘELECKÝ ISLAND**
Old Town ①

There is a small sandy beach on the northern tip, a unique spot where the river sings louder than the city. The spired building on the right bank is home to the museum of Bedřich Smetana, a composer who was inspired by the Vltava River for his famous symphonic poem.

427 **ŠTVANICE**
Holešovice ⑥

A busy motorway cuts through this island, which was traditionally devoted to sports. Prague's oldest tennis club is here as well as a white water training facility and a bicross track. The slightly run-down villa next to it, which dates from 1824, has a bar where alternative theatre performances are organised.

428 **CÍSAŘSKÝ ISLAND**
Troja ⑩

Half of this island is occupied by water treatment plants, the other half belongs to horses. Situated between the Royal Game Reserve and Troja, it is a perfect place to ride out. Confident riders (only!) can book a horse with Mr Václav Koudela (+420 603 174 039) for 600 CZK an hour.

429 LIBEŇSKÝ ISLAND
Libeň

From Libeňský Bridge head down the cycling trail for about 500 metres, leaving the sculptor's studio on your right and the community gardens on your left behind you. Find a quirky secret bar at the end of a narrow footpath where you can enjoy a beer (*Yedno pheevo*) or a refreshing raspberry soda (*mullinofka*).

430 SLOVANSKÝ ISLAND
New Town ②

Also called Žofín, after a neo-Renaissance palace. In 1841, the first Czech-made steam engine was demonstrated here. Today, a miniature kids' minitrain runs on the 53-metre-long railway near the playground. There is a fountain with drinking water nearby. Alcohol consumption is banned in the park.

426 STŘELECKÝ ISLAND

The 5 most interesting
SUBURBS TO EXPLORE

431 **JIŽNÍ MĚSTO**
(Opatov metro station)

Walk east through Prague's Central Park, a green strip with verges for sound isolation between the panel housing estate built in 1980s. Soon you will catch a glimpse of grey twin towers with a yellow clock. Kupa restaurant, which is on the 22nd floor, has a spectacular view of Prague and its surroundings.

432 **ŽIŽKOV**
(Jiřího z Poděbrad metro station)

A neighbourhood of many contrasts. The area near the TV tower is very residential, elegant and green. As you walk down the hill, the streets become narrower and dirtier and the bars dodgier. The statue in Kostnické Square usually holds a beer barrel during festivals. The street names are linked to the Czech Reformation movement.

433 **MALVAZINKY**

(Malvazinky bus stop)

⑦

After WWI, the municipality launched a social housing project, which transformed into one of the most picturesque corners of Prague. Přímá and Pravoúhlá Streets will charm you with their tiny terraced houses and pocket-size gardens. Take a short excursion to Paví Vrch lookout and make your way back downhill through Santoška Park.

434 **KRÁLOVSKÉ VINOHRADY**

(Vinohradská vodárna tram stop)

④

Admire the ornate water tower that has been converted into apartments. Walk downhill to Hus Congregational House, a church built in the purist style of the 1930s, from which Czech Radio broadcast during WWII until the liberation. There are some spectacular villas on Dykova, Hradešínská and Na Šafránce (such as the Šaloun Atelier).

435 **BABA**

(Nádraží Podbaba tram stop)

Perched on a rocky promontory, this unique residential district is teeming with Functionalist villas. It takes its name from the romantic ruin by the cliff. Start in Nad Paťankou Street and admire the bright cubic shapes and the majestic terraces with their spectacular views.

5 great places to
COOL DOWN IN THE SUMMER

436 PETYNKA SWIMMING POOL

Otevřená 4
Střešovice ③
+420 235 094 068
koupalistepetynka.cz

The most centrally-located outdoor pool in town, from where you can even see Prague Castle. It has a slide, beach volleyball, ping-pong and a paddling pool for children. Swimming for an hour costs 60 CZK, a ticket for the day will set you back 160 CZK.

437 LAKE HOSTIVAŘ

K Jezeru
Hostivař
+420 777 609 859
hostivarskapreshrada.cz

Prague's largest lake, which is very popular with the locals year round, with a long sandy beach, plenty of grassy knolls and verges and a nudist beach. Easy to get to by public transport. You can rent boats, kayaks and pedal boats or just chill with a cocktail. Entry fees vary between 20 and 90 CZK.

438 POND PODLESÁK

Uhříněves

In the middle of Říčanka natural reserve lies a pond with grassy banks and a dam with centenary oak trees, with a nature trail. It is a 45-minute walk from Uhříněves train station, so a car might be a better option on a hot day.

439 BIOTOP RADOTÍN

K Lázním 9
Radotín
+420 774 485 998
biotopradotin.cz

The first natural swimming pool in Prague without chlorine. It relies on a biological method to keep the water clean, with the help of aquatic plants and natural ecosystems. The two kidney-shaped lakes (one for bathing, one for cleaning) were created following the redevelopment of a former brown-field.

440 LAKE KŘENEK

Ovčáry

After decades of gravel mining, Křenek hill became a gorgeous lake with sandy beaches surrounded by a pine forest. If you're up for a thrill, try your hand at water skiing. It is outside Prague, so you need a car to get there.

440 LAKE KŘENEK

The 5 best ways to

GET FIT

441 **BIKE ALONG BEROUNKA RIVER**

Rent a bike at Smíchov train station (150 CZK per day, 1000 CZK deposit, two proofs of identity needed) and hop on board of any train to Beroun. Get off at Karlštejn and make your way back through the winding Berounka River valley.

442 **MAMUT CLIMBING HALL**
Bubenská 43
Holešovice ⑧
+420 233 371 481
stenaholesovice.cz

One of the largest climbing facilities in the country, with five halls and a total surface area of 2600 sqm. Professionals and (less) skilled amateurs can find a wall that matches their capacities, the tallest being 12 metres. They rent out all the necessary equipment and teach classes, of course.

443 **LADRONKA**
Tomanova 1
Břevnov ③
+420 601 584 223
ladronka.com

Arguably the best roller skating trail in town, situated on a plateau with panoramic views and a fresh breeze. You can find a rental store midway along the 4-kilometre trail, which has all kinds of inline and roller skates, scooters and skateboards. Two proofs of identity and a cash deposit required.

444 VÝLETNÁ

Letenské sady 32
Holešovice ⑧
+420 778 542 712
www.vyletna.info

A regeneration project, which succeeded thanks to the combined efforts of local volunteers. The very affordable bar is a source of income for further works. They have several tennis courts, a ping-pong table and a foosball table. A cosy feel. Kept by a group of enthusiasts who refuse to let this heritage perish.

445 VODÁCKÝ RÁJ

Císařská louka 27
Smíchov ⑦
+420 257 215 439
vodackyraj.cz

Here they rent out kayaks, canoes and rafts for up to 9 people, including all the accessories. In Prague you can row until Jiráskův Bridge (where the first barrage is located), or upstream as far as you please. They also provide information about the water conditions on other rivers.

443 **LADRONKA**

5 cool places for an ADVENTURE

446 **PATER NOSTER ELEVATOR**
AT: YMCA PALACE
Na Poříčí 12
New Town ①

This elevator, which is open to the public, consists of a chain of open compartments that move slowly in a loop. It also goes by a very dramatic name: 'the elevator of death'. Most people wonder what happens after the top and bottom floor. Nothing dangerous of course, but after this experience you will be able to share your insightful testimony with your friends.

447 **BREAKOUT ESCAPE GAME**
Husinecká 25
Žižkov ⑤
+420 777 312 356
breakoutprague.com

1950s Czechoslovakia. The world was teetering on the brink of the Cold War. You have sixty minutes to find documents that have been hidden by the resistance in a nuclear fallout shelter, before the secret police do. Your success (or failure?) will have a dramatic impact on political developments in the Eastern Bloc...

448 BOBSLED RUN/BOBOVÁ DRÁHA PROSEK

Prosecká 34b
Vysočany
+420 284 840 520
bobovadraha.cz

An 800-metre-long steel chute for courageous kids and playful adults who enjoy a bit of fun. The speed can be easily controlled by using the brake but feel free to ignore it and scream at the top of your lungs. There is also a 5-metre-high rope park, a smaller one for children and a trampoline.

449 MERCURIA LASER GAME

Argentinská 38
Holešovice ⑧
+420 605 111 811
mercurialaser.cz

No need to worry about bruises in this dark maze, which is located in an old warehouse. This is the largest arena in town covering a surface area of 400 sqm. Select one of ten different game modes and fight individually or in a team to collect points and win a free drink.

450 FLIGHT SIMULATOR

Zborovská 47
Smíchov ⑦
+420 228 882 287
flyipilot.com

Here you won't hear "Hello, this is your captain speaking" over the intercom. Because here you are the pilot. Sit in the cockpit of an Airbus 320-passenger jet, take off in London and land in Hong Kong, struggle through a storm or engine failure. Special programmes to tackle fear of flying are also available.

The 5 best places for a
ROMANTIC DATE

451 **DEER MOAT**
Chotkova
Lesser Town ③

Follow the main road until you reach a gate, then walk across the ravine over what resembles narrow scaffolding. Enjoy the dim light of the tunnel, imagine the deer that used to roam here and then look for the Masaryk lookout, which offers an amazing view of the castle minus the crowds.

452 **MARKÉTSKÁ GARDEN**
Markétská 1
Břevnov ③

This is where the university students, whose dorms are next door, like to go for romantic dates. Start near the small ponds in the front, then make your way through the monastery to the *orangerie*, which boasts some charming olive trees and recent art in the Entrance gallery (open Thursday to Sunday).

453 **HAVLÍČKOVY SADY**
Koperníkova
Vinohrady ④

Enter the park at the top of the street. You will find yourself between the waterfall and the artificial grotto, in front of which stands a fountain with a statue of Neptune. Bring a bottle of Italian wine for a real taste of *la dolce vita*.

454 MIRROR MAZE

Petřínské sady
Lesser Town ③
+420 724 911 497
petrinska-rozhledna.cz

A wooden labyrinth that was built for the 1891 Prague Exhibition is hidden in a castle-like building, near Petřín Tower (measured from the river and including the hill, it is just as high as the Eiffel Tower). Head for the last part with its magic mirrors to test your date's sense of humour.

455 SEMINARY GARDEN

Hellichova
Lesser Town ③

The sunny slopes of Petřín hill have always been associated with love, whose symbol – a statue of Karel Hynek Mácha, the Czech Republic's greatest Romantic poet – stands in this very park. The most charming part is the Seminary Garden, especially in spring when the cherry trees flower.

455 SEMINARY GARDEN

5 fun

TRIPS OUTSIDE PRAGUE

456 **POSÁZAVSKÝ PACIFIK**

The charming meanders of the Sázava River are best explored by train. Nostalgic steam trains are sometimes used, but a regular engine-powered locomotive can do the trick too. Get off at Český Šternberk to see the castle, at Rataje for the woodcutting museum or at Sázava for a swim in the river by the monastery. It takes 1 hour and 30 min by train, one change at Čerčany.

457 **TÁBOR**

Back in the day the military camp of the Hussite Reformist movement used to be located here. A delightful town with romantic alleys and town houses, which is home to the Hussite museum, underground tunnels and Kotnov Tower, a remnant of a fortified castle. If you wish to spend the night, check out the Dvořák Hotel (www.dvoraktabor.cz). One hour and 20 minutes by train.

458 CHATEAU KONOPIŠTĚ

Konopiště 1
Benešov
+420 317 721 366
zamek-konopiste.cz

Konopiště was the home of the passionate hunter Franz Ferdinand d'Este, whose assassination led to the beginning of WWI. It is just a 2-kilometre walk from the lovely train station, which boasts a Kaiser Salon (for when his uncle came to visit), most of it through the castle park. It takes 1 hour by train to Benešov.

459 CHATEAU DOBŘÍŠ

Náměstí Svobody 1
Dobříš
+420 318 521 240
zamekdobris.cz

The town of Dobříš is very proud of its French-style Chateau, which used to belong to the Writers' Association. It is surrounded by a beautiful garden and an English park with lakes. Have a lunch at U Tří statkářů or spend the night in the castle hotel. Only 40 minutes by bus.

460 BOHEMIAN PARADISE

This fairy-tale-like nature reserve with bizarre rock formations, vantage points and majestic castles among deep pine forests absolutely resembles paradise. An area of stunning natural beauty and a perfect campsite. More demanding travellers will be happy to hear Hrubá Skála Chateau is a luxury hotel (www.hrubaskala.cz). It takes 2 hours by train to Turnov-Město.

K10

40 RANDOM FACTS AND URBAN DETAILS

The 5 coolest workplaces for FREELANCERS

461 **NODE5**
Radlická 50
Smíchov ⑦
+420 776 140 985
node5.cz

A community of talent works on this factory floor. Attracting (future) start-up founders, hackers and tech superstars, they aim to start a co-working revolution. If you are searching for an inspiring alternative vibe, look no further and book your spot, including a mentoring programme.

462 **OPERO**
Salvátorská 8
Old Town ①
+420 777 167 376
opero.cz

This premium co-working space is located just around the corner from the Old Town Square. Tucked away in a courtyard of a former printer's that underwent a very gentle renovation, the sleek design of its open-space premises is just terrific.

463 **K10**
Koperníkova 10
Vinohrady ④
+420 775 898 761
k10.online

On a southern slope of Vinohrady, you will find this majestic villa with its lovely garden. Whether you take it easy working a maximum of 50 hours per month or have a tendency to be a workaholic, they have the right membership formula. Or else just rent a jaw-dropping meeting room to impress your guests.

464 PAPER HUB

Dělnická 43
Holešovice ⑧
+420 774 670 783
paperhub.cz

On the first floor above Parallel Polis cafe, a haven for crypto-anarchists. If you fall for it during your free one-day trial, you will be asked to pay for your membership in Bitcoins. Expect an uber-safe internet connection, high-tech office equipment and a free ticket to the hackers' conference that is organised here regularly.

465 FORBIDDEN SPOT

Bubenská 1
Bubny ⑧
+420 731 910 446
forbiddenspot.com

Ring the bell to enter the art gallery and studio of *Life is Porno* creations. Everything is completely covered in paint and graffiti, including the furniture and toilets. Another door then gives out into a generous open office lounge with hammocks, a water bed and a candy bar.

463 **K10**

5 clever

MONEY-SAVING TIPS

466 AIRPORT TRANSPORT

Like everywhere else, airport taxis are predators. Try to resist the urge and choose one of the easy, fast and cheap ways to get to and from the airport instead. The 119 bus combined with the A (green) metro line will take you downtown for 32 CZK. If you want to avoid having to switch then catch the Airport Express bus to the main train station for 60 CZK.

467 MONEY EXCHANGE

Kaprova 13
Old Town ①
+420 200 700 890
exchange.cz

To avoid scams think twice before exchanging your money, pay special attention to the commission and the exchange rate. Fair exchange offices, such as Exchange ask 0% and will give you at least 25 CZK for 1 euro. For current rates, check the website of the Czech National Bank (www.cnb.cz) before your trip.

468 **TAP WINES**

No need to pay a fortune for some good Moravian wine, as most *vinotékas* will sell you a bottle, which is tapped directly from the barrel. A litre of decent table wine will set you back about 2 to 3 euros. A few reliable choices: Víno z Podskalí (Podskalská 13, New Town) or Koštovna u Počtů (Milady Horákové 47, Holešovice).

469 **FREE CLASSICAL MUSIC**

Malostranské náměstí 13
Lesser Town ③
+420 234 244 111
www.hamu.cz

There is a free graduation ceremony concert open to the public at HAMU (Music and Dance Faculty of the Performing Arts Academy) almost every day. They usually start around 7.30 pm but we recommend checking the programme just outside the gate to be on the safe side. Then slip through the courtyard, follow the arrows and the sound of French horn or piano.

470 **WATER**

Prague's tap water is of very good quality and perfectly drinkable. In the city alone there are about twenty public drinking water-fountains. When ordering in a restaurant and asking for tap water, they may charge you a small fee for a large carafe, but it will always be much less than the price of bottled water.

The 5 most useful
WEBSITES AND APPS

471 **PUBLIC TRANSPORT**
www.idos.cz
Jízdní řády IDOS (app)

Need to check your train, tram or ferry timetable? This integrated website has all the data you need, on an English or German user-friendly platform, and also indicates the price most of the time. Public transport is an efficient and cheap way to get around, and also offers plenty of opportunities to observe the locals in their habitat.

472 **BLUE ANGEL TAXI**
Modrý anděl (app)

If you prefer to travel by taxi, try to avoid hailing a taxi on the street, as the risk of scams is higher. While (pre)ordering your ride, the app will give you a price estimate and suggest an itinerary, which you can show to the driver. You can request a car with a credit card terminal.

473 **GO OUT**

goout.net

Also available as an app, this website keeps tabs on all the interesting cultural events that take place in the capital. Search the dates, venues or artists you are interested in. Last but not least, they publish inspiring articles about various parts of town with plenty of useful tips for discoveries.

474 **OFFLINE MAPS**

mapy.cz

To save on roaming charges or mobile data (and to avoid racking up a huge bill), download an offline map of the Czech Republic. The whole package is almost half a gigabyte, but will provide you with sufficient details about the city but also for hikes in the countryside or the mountains.

475 **CZECH TOURIST CLUB**

trasy.kct.cz

The Czechs have a long-standing hiking tradition. One tip is to get off the train in any station and simply follow a signposted route to another public transport hub. Prefer to plan ahead? Check the online planner to map out your hike, making sure not to miss anything interesting along the way.

5 important

DATES IN RECENT HISTORY

476 **16 MAY 1868**

Was the day when the foundation stone of the National Theatre building was laid, an important moment in the process of Czech cultural emancipation from the German-speaking Empire. Its construction, which for the greater part was financed with public funds, took thirteen years. Four months later the theatre burned down.

477 **28 OCTOBER 1918**

After several efforts at federalisation and long negotiations during WWI, the victorious Allies agreed to the foundation of a new Czechoslovak Republic. On this day, the declaration of independence was signed in Prague, with Tomáš Garrigue Masaryk serving as the first president of the new state.

478 **20 AUGUST 1968**

On a balmy summer's night, the armies of the Warsaw Pact crossed the borders of the Czechoslovak Republic. This invasion put an end to the liberalisation reforms of Alexander Dubček, consolidating Soviet authority. Tens of thousands of citizens fled the country soon after.

479 **17 NOVEMBER 1989**

That year thousands of people joined in the celebrations of International Student Day. After the violent suppression of the peaceful march, a rumour spread that the police had shot a young medical student, enraging the population. Every day more and more people joined the protest, until the government caved in, sealing the fall of the Iron Curtain.

480 **AUGUST 2002**

The unremitting rains of summer 2002 caused huge floods in the Czech Republic. The capital was heavily affected, the Vltava's flow rate was a hundred times higher than average. Prague's metro, the ZOO and Karlín district were submerged, forcing the country to tackle its flood prevention, which was found to be sorely lacking.

5 homes of

FAMOUS PEOPLE

481 **ALBERT EINSTEIN**
Lesnická 7
Smíchov ⑦

The Einsteins spent just 18 months in this riverside house. In 1911, Smíchov was a brand-new neighbourhood, just a 15-minute-ride to the university where the great physicist had been working on his relativity theory. Prague seemed to have provided some much-needed composure for his scientific research, but far less so for his marital life.

482 **JOHANNES KEPLER**
Karlova 4
Old Town ①

This small detour provides a welcome relief from the maddening crowds. Turn into the courtyard of Karlova no. 4 to discover Renaissance arcades and a small museum about its famous resident who lived here in the 1600s. It takes just 30 minutes of your time and 2 euros to remind you about the discoveries of this famous astronomer.

483 W.A. MOZART

Vila Bertramka
Mozartova 169
Smíchov ⑦

Surrounded by woods, this former farmstead belonged to the Dušek family, who regularly received Mozart when he stayed in Prague. He is said to have finished composing his most famous opera *Don Giovanni* here in 1787.

484 VÁCLAV HAVEL

Rašínovo nábřeží 78
New Town ②

Next to the Dancing House stands a building by Havel's great-grandfather. With its large windows and spacious loggias, it was clearly influenced by Parisian architecture. Václav was born on the fourth floor and spent most of his life there (even as president). Evidence exists that he was being spied on by the secret police from the nearby Šítkovská Tower.

485 ALFONS MUCHA

Thunovská 25
Lesser Town ③

The apartment of this famous Czech painter, graphic artist and active freemason was located just under the castle stairs. He lived here from 1911 till 1923, and regularly travelled to Zbiroh Castle, where his most important work – *The Slav Epic* – came to life. This cycle of 20 large canvases depicts the mythology and history of the Czechs.

5
METRO STATIONS
worth visiting

486 **FLORENC**
METRO C

In the southern hall of the red metro a 7-metre-long mosaic commemorates the Battle at Sokolovo, where Czechoslovak legions fought together with the Red Army in 1943. A Czech-Italian duo from the Academy of Fine Arts collected colourful stones from all over the country. It is the very first work of art in the Prague metro.

487 **MALOSTRANSKÁ**
METRO A

Frequented by tourists, yet they often fail to notice the local statues. They're all copies of Mathias Braun's allegorical series of *Virtues and Vices*. The first stands at the top of the escalators. A young woman looking towards heaven for salvation and holding an anchor is the depiction of Hope. There are more in the garden.

488 **ANDĚL**
METRO B

Above the southern escalator a pink marble will catch your attention. A branch of lilacs, the Soviet symbol of peace and partnership, connects two words: Moskva - Praha. Formerly called Moskevská, this station was twinned with a station in the Russian capital. Its counterpart, Prazhskaya station, can still be found in Moscow's southern suburbs.

489 **VLTAVSKÁ**
METRO C

Digging metro tunnels under the river was quite a technical feat in 1984. Which is why the decorations are an allegory of a watercourse. Today *Faun and Vltava* have sadly lost most of their glory, but travellers used to be hugely impressed by the 8-metre-high cascade.

490 **MŮSTEK**
METRO B

A mosaic mural decorates the hall leading to Jungmannovo Square. It depicts a walk through Prague, meeting writers and lovers on an imaginary route from the National Museum to the National Theatre and across the Charles Bridge. Prague's coat of arms however leaves no doubts about which city this is.

5 *famous*
MOVIE LOCATIONS

491 **SAINT GILES CHURCH**
AMADEUS, 1984
Husova 8
Old Town ①

The Oscar-winning American filmmaker of Czech origin, Miloš Forman, chose to film Mozart's wedding in this Baroque church. The backdrop of the splendid gilded altar certainly looked amazing in this biopic film about the musical genius who was portrayed as 'an unprincipled spoilt conceited brat'.

492 **CHOTKOVA-BADENIHO JUNCTION**
ANTHROPOID, 2016
Hradčany ③

Inspired by a true story of a WWII resistance operation to assassinate one of the main architects of the Holocaust and the acting Protector of Bohemia and Moravia. Not the original location of the 27 May 1942 event, but more suited as a movie set thanks to the well preserved surroundings.

493 **DANUBE HOUSE**

CASINO ROYALE, 2006

Rohanské nábřeží 2

Karlín ⑥

The black and white opening scene was filmed in this high-rise building. Bond breaks into Dryden's office to find out that the second killing is 'considerably' easier. An action that earns him a licence to kill and his status as an 00 agent.

494 **THE PRAGUE ZOO**

THE ZOOKEEPER'S WIFE, 2017

U Trojského zámku 3

Troja ⑩⑧

Allegedly set in Poland, this true story was almost entirely shot in and around Prague's ZOO and exhibition grounds. The stars of the movie were Jessica Chastain and Tamara and Janita, two Sri Lankan female elephants. It tells the tale of the zookeeper's wife's courage as she hid Jewish fugitives during WWII.

495 **VINOHRADY THEATRE**

THE ILLUSIONIST, 2006

Náměstí Míru 7

Vinohrady ④

The neo-Renaissance façade of Vinohrady's Náměstí míru was where Edward Norton as Eisenheim staged a magic show involving necromancy. Did his performance really unlock mysteries and bend nature's laws, or was it merely an illusion?

5 random

URBAN DETAILS

496 **GAS STREET LAMPS**

Three remnants of the pre-electric street lighting system can be found in three squares: Dražického, Hradčanské and Loretto Square. These charming cast-iron structures cast a greenish light and make a low humming sound. In the old days they were turned on and off one by one by a lamplighter with a special long hook.

497 **CABRIO TRAM**
www.facebook.com/mazacitramvaj

A red vehicle marked M can be seen in any part of town, at any time of the day. Its main job is to grease the rails. In winter times it is equipped with a snow plough and sometimes carries Christmas decorations. Apart from a Facebook fan page it also has a real-time web camera.

498 **STREET NUMBERING**

Double street numbering in Prague can be rather confusing, with its red and blue numbers. The former is usually longer and refers to the cadastre log (for each municipality), the latter is used for orientation within each street or square (and is used in this guide).

499 STREET PIANOS

piananaulici.cz

Everything started in the summer of 2013, when the first five pianos were installed in the streets of Prague as a citizen's initiative. The objective was to make people pause in public space, to play or to listen and interact. Soon chessboards were added as the project spread to 50 other Czech cities.

500 NA OVOCE

na-ovoce.cz

Urban dwellers tend to be rather detached from nature, which is why this project, that aims to popularise Prague's orchards, was launched to help people be aware of the seasonal rhythms through fruit trees. A user-friendly map will show you where to go to collect fruit and herbs nearby, you can add your own tips too.

499 STREET PIANOS

INDEX

COLOPHON

EDITING AND COMPOSING – Vendula Havlikova

GRAPHIC DESIGN – Joke Gossé and Tinne Luyten

PHOTOGRAPHY – Zbyněk Riedl - www.zbynekriedl.cz

COVER IMAGE – Nákladové nádraží Žižkov (secret 266)

The addresses in this book have been selected after thorough independent research by the author, in collaboration with Luster Publishers. The selection is solely based on personal evaluation of the business by the author. Nothing in this book was published in exchange for payment or benefits of any kind.

D/2017/12.005/11
ISBN 978 94 6058 2103
NUR 510, 512

www.lusterweb.com – www.the500hiddensecrets.com
info@lusterweb.com

Printed in Italy by Printer Trento.

FSC www.fsc.org MIX Paper from responsible sources FSC® C015829